SALVAT(

MW01116368

ENGLISH - ITA

Your Essential Travel Guide Book about Italy:
Learn Italian with Common Phrases for Everyday Use,
Bilingual Insights, and Phonetics for Easy Communication

**PHRASES SUITABLE FOR EVERYONE
WITH CHAPTERS DEDICATED TO:**

TURI PAPALE

*Traveling to Italy should be a joy, not a stress.
With this phrasebook, you'll navigate your Italian adventure effortlessly,
enjoying every moment without the language barrier.
Make the most of your trip with confidence and ease!*

Disclaimer

The author and publisher of this book disclaim any liability for any direct, indirect, incidental, or consequential damages or losses that may result from the use or misuse of the information, expressions, or content provided in this book. This book is provided "as is," and while efforts have been made to ensure the accuracy and relevancy of the content, the author and publisher make no representations or warranties of any kind regarding the completeness, accuracy, reliability, suitability, or availability with respect to the book or the information contained within for any purpose.

Users of this book are advised to use their judgment and discretion in their communications. The phrases and language tips provided herein are intended as a guide only and should not be construed as professional language training or deeply culturally comprehensive advice. Any reliance on place on such information is therefore strictly at your own risk.

In no event will the author or the publisher be liable for any loss or damage including without limitation, indirect or consequential loss or damage, or any loss or damage arising from loss of data or profits arising out of, or in connection with, theuse of this book.

This disclaimer does not negate any statutory warranties or rights that cannot be excluded under applicable law.

Preface

Unlock the Secrets of Everyday Italian with Ease!
Are you planning a trip to Italy for business, leisure, or a permanent move? Are you worried about navigating daily interactions in a foreign language?This book is your essential companion, designed to address all your concerns and make your experience in Italy smooth and enjoyable.

Why Choose This Book?
1. **Comprehensive and Up-to-date:** Unlike outdated phrasebooks,this guide offers fresh, relevant phrases for modern-day scenarios. Whether you are dining out, asking for directions, or dealing with emergencies, you will find the exact phrases you need.

2. **Specialized Phrases:** We understand that everyone has unique needs. That is why we have included specific sections for:
   - People with celiac disease and Gluten-Free Diets
   - Dairy-Free Diet
   - Nut-Free Diet
   - Vegans and Vegetarians Diets
   - Wheelchair Users

3. **Ease of Use:** Each Italian phrase is paired with its English translation. If you cannot pronounce the Italian word, just point to it. Italians are known for their warmth and hospitality,and they will appreciate your effort, even if your accent is not perfect.

4. **Built for Real-Life Situations:** Beyond basic introductions and common restaurant dialogues, this book prepares you for a variety of situations that other guides often overlook.

Peace of Mind in Emergencies:
In a crisis, clear communication is crucial. This book ensures you can convey your needs quickly and accurately, helping you stay calm and find assistance promptly.

Why You will Love It:
- **Practical:** Tailored for real-life use, ensuring you have the right words at the right time.
- **Supportive:** Encourages you to engage with locals confidently, knowing you have a reliable tool at your fingertips.
- **Inclusive:** Addresses the needs of diverse travellers, ensuring everyone feels catered to.

Phonetic Guide to Italian Pronunciation for English Speakers

Italian is a language known for its melodic flow and clear pronunciation. For English speakers, mastering Italian pronunciation can enhance the communication experience while visiting Italy. This chapter provides a phoneticguide to help you pronounce Italian words correctly, with examples for each letter of the Italian alphabet.

A - [ah]
Example: Amore (Love)
ah-MOH-reh

B - [bee]
Example: Bambino (Child)
bahn-BEE-noh

C - [chee] before I or E, [kah] otherwise
Example: Ciao (Hello); Carro (Car)
CHEE-ow; KAH-rro

D - [dee]
Example: Domani (Tomorrow)
doh-MAH-nee

E - [eh]
Example: Elefante (Elephant)
eh-leh-FAHN-teh

F - [effe]
Example: Formaggio (Cheese)
for-MAH-jjoh

G - [jee] before I or E, [gah] otherwise
Example: Gelato (Ice cream); Gatto (Cat)
jeh-LAH-toh; GAHT-toh

H - [acca] (always silent)
Example: Hotel
oh-TEL

I - [ee]
Example: Isola (Island)
EE-so-lah

J - [i lunga] (rare, mostly in loanwords)
Example: Jeans
JEANS (same as English)

K - [kappa] (rare, used mainly in foreign words)
Example: Kiwi
KEE-wee

L - [elle]
Example: Luce (Light)
LOO-che

M - [emme]
Example: Mondo (World)
MOHN-doh

N - [enne]
Example: Notte (Night)
NOHT-teh

O - [oh]
Example: Oro (Gold)
OH-roh

P - [pee]
Example: Pizza
PEE-tzah

Q - [koo]
Example: Quota (Quote)
KWO-tah

R - [erre] (rolled R)
Example: Rosso (Red)
ROHS-soh

S - [esse]
Example: Sole (Sun)
SOH-leh

T - [tee]
Example: Tempo (Time)
TEHM-poh

U - [oo]
Example: Uva (Grape)
OO-vah

V - [voo]
Example: Vino (Wine)
VEE-noh

W - [doppia vu] (used mainly in foreign words)
Example: Water (used in some Italian menus for water)
WAH-ter

X - [iks] (rare, used mainly in loanwords and proper nouns)
Example: Xilofono (Xylophone)
zee-LOH-fo-no

Y - [ipsilon] (rare, used mainly in loanwords)
Example: Yogurt
YOH-goort

Z - [zeta]
Example: Zebra
DZEH-brah

This phonetic guide should serve as a helpful tool in your journey to learn Italian, making it easier to pronounce words accurately and thereby enhancing your communication and experience in Italy. Enjoy your linguistic adventure!

Colors *Colori*

Red - rosso - *roh-soh*
Blue - blu - *blu*
Green - verde - *vehr-deh*
Yellow - giallo - *jahl-loh*
Black - nero - *neh-roh*
White - bianco - *bee-an-koh*
Orange - arancione - *ah-rahn-choh-neh*
Purple - viola - *vee-oh-lah*
Pink - rosa - *roh-zah*
Brown - marrone - *mahr-roh-neh*

Numbers *Numeri*

One - uno - *oo-noh*
Two - due - *doo-eh*
Three - tre - *treh*
Four - quattro - *kwah-troh*
Five - cinque - *cheen-kweh*
Six - sei - *say*
Seven - sette - *seh-teh*
Eight - otto - *oh-toh*
Nine - nove - *noh-veh*
Ten - dieci - *dee-eh-chee*

Days of the Week *Giorni della Settimana*

Monday - lunedì - *loo-neh-dee*
Tuesday - martedì - *mahr-teh-dee*
Wednesday - mercoledì - *mehr-koh-leh-dee*
Thursday - giovedì - *joh-veh-dee*
Friday - venerdì - *veh-nehr-dee*
Saturday - sabato - *sah-bah-toh*
Sunday - domenica - *doh-meh-nee-kah*

Months of the Year *Mesi dell'Anno*

January - gennaio - *jehn-nah-yoh*
February - febbraio - *fehb-brah-yoh*
March - marzo - *mahr-tsoh*
April - aprile - *ah-pree-leh*
May - maggio - *mahj-joh*
June - giugno - *joo-nyoh*
July - luglio - *loo-lyoh*
August - agosto - *ah-goh-stoh*
September - settembre - *seht-tehm-breh*
October - ottobre - *oh-toh-breh*
November - novembre - *noh-vehm-breh*
December - dicembre - *dee-chem-breh*

Airport

How do I get to the airport?
Come faccio ad arrivare in aeroporto?
Koh-meh fah-tcho ad ah-rree-vah-reh een ah-eh-roh-por-toh?

What time does the airport shuttle leave?
A che ora parte la navetta per l'aeroporto?
Ah keh oh-rah par-teh lah nah-veh-tah pehr l'ah-eh-roh-por-toh?

Where can I check-in for my flight?
Dove posso fare il check-in per il mio volo?
Doh-veh pohs-soh fah-reh eel chehk-een pehr eel mee-oh voh-loh?

Can you call a taxi to the airport?
Puoi chiamare un taxi per l'aeroporto?
Pwoh-ee kee-ah-mah-reh oon tahk-see pehr l'ah-eh-roh-por-toh?

How early should I arrive at the airport?
Quanto prima dovrei arrivare in aeroporto?
Kwahn-toh pree-mah doh-vreh-ee ah-rree-vah-reh een ah-eh-roh-por-toh?

Is there a direct bus to the airport?
C'è un autobus diretto per l'aeroporto?
Cheh oon ow-toh-boos dee-reht-toh pehr l'ah-eh-roh-por-toh?

How much is the taxi fare to the airport?
Quanto costa il taxi per l'aeroporto?
Kwahn-toh koh-stah eel tahk-see pehr l'ah-eh-roh-por-toh?

Where is the airport check-in desk?
Dove si trova il banco check-in dell'aeroporto?
Doh-veh see troh-vah eel bahn-koh chehk-een dehl-l'ah-eh-roh-por-toh?

Can I get a map of the airport?
Posso avere una mappa dell'aeroporto?
Pohs-soh ah-veh-reh oo-nah mahp-pah dehl-l'ah-eh-roh-por-toh?

What time is the last call for my flight?
Qual è l'ultimo avviso per il mio volo?
Kwah-leh l'ool-tee-moh ah-vee-zoh pehr eel mee-oh voh-loh?

Where is the nearest airport exit?
Dove è l'uscita più vicina dell'aeroporto?
Doh-veh eh l'oo-shee-tah pyoo vee-chee-nah dehl-l'ah-eh-roh-por-toh?

Can I have some water, please?
Posso avere dell'acqua, per favore?
Pohs-soh ah-veh-reh dehl-l'ah-kwah, pehr fah-voh-reh?

Where can I find a luggage cart?
Dove posso trovare un carrello per i bagagli?
Doh-veh pohs-soh troh-vah-reh oon kahr-rehl-loh pehr ee bah-gahl-yee?

Is there a currency exchange in the airport?
C'è un cambio valuta in aeroporto?
Cheh oon kahm-bee-oh vah-loo-tah een ah-eh-roh-por-toh?

Where is the lost and found?
Dove si trova l'oggetto smarrito?
Doh-veh see troh-vah l'ohj-geht-toh smahr-ree-toh?

13

How do I connect to the airport Wi-Fi?
Come faccio a connettermi al Wi-Fi dell'aeroporto?
Koh-meh fah-tcho ah kon-neh-tehr-mee ahl Wee-Fee dehl-l'ah-eh-roh-por-toh?

Can you help me with my luggage?
Puoi aiutarmi con i miei bagagli?
Pwoh-ee ah-yoo-tahr-mee kon ee mee-eh-ee bah-gahl-yee?

Where can I buy a ticket for the airport bus?
Dove posso comprare un biglietto per l'autobus dell'aeroporto?
Doh-veh pohs-soh kohm-prah-reh oon bee-lyeh-toh pehr low-toh-boos dehl-l'ah-eh-roh-por-toh?

Do I need to recheck my bags?
Devo riconsegnare i miei bagagli?
Deh-voh ree-kohn-sehn-yah-reh ee mee-eh-ee bah-gahl-yee?

Where is the boarding gate?
Dove è il gate di imbarco?
Doh-veh eh eel gah-teh dee eem-bahr-koh?

Are You Up for...?

Would you like to have a coffee?
Ti va di prendere un caffè?
Tee vah dee prehn-deh-reh oon kahf-feh?

Would you like to go for a walk?
Ti va di fare una passeggiata?
Tee vah dee fah-reh oo-nah pahs-seh-jee-ah-tah?

Would you like to visit a museum?
Ti va di visitare un museo?
Tee vah dee vee-zee-tah-reh oon moo-seh-oh?

Would you like to eat something?
Ti va di mangiare qualcosa?
Tee vah dee man-jah-reh kwahl-koh-sah?

Would you like to watch a movie?
Ti va di vedere un film?
Tee vah dee veh-deh-reh oon feelm?

Would you like to go shopping?
Ti va di andare a fare shopping?
Tee vah dee ahn-dah-reh ah fah-reh shop-ping?

Would you like to try some local food?
Ti va di provare del cibo locale?
Tee vah dee proh-vah-reh del chee-boh loh-kah-leh?

Would you like to take a picture?
Ti va di fare una foto?
Tee vah dee fah-reh oo-nah foh-toh?

Would you like to go to the beach?
Ti va di andare in spiaggia?
Tee vah dee ahn-dah-reh een spee-ah-jah?

Would you like to have an ice cream?
Ti va di mangiare un gelato?
Tee vah dee man-jah-reh oon jeh-lah-toh?

Would you like to have a drink?
Ti va di prendere qualcosa da bere?
Tee vah dee prehn-deh-reh kwahl-koh-sah dah beh-reh?

Would you like to dance?
Ti va di ballare?
Tee vah dee bah-lah-reh?

Would you like to go to a concert?
Ti va di andare a un concerto?
Tee vah dee ahn-dah-reh ah oon kon-cher-toh?

Would you like to ride a bike?
Ti va di andare in bicicletta?
Tee vah dee ahn-dah-reh een bee-chee-klet-tah?

Would you like to cook together?
Ti va di cucinare insieme?
Tee vah dee koo-chee-nah-reh een-syeh-meh?

Would you like to learn Italian?
Ti va di imparare l'italiano?
Tee vah dee eem-pah-rah-reh lee-tah-lyah-noh?

Would you like to go to the opera?
Ti va di andare all'opera?
Tee vah dee ahn-dah-reh ahl-loh-peh-rah?

Would you like to go out tonight?
Ti va di uscire stasera?
Tee vah dee oos-chee-reh stah-seh-rah?

Would you like to explore the city?
Ti va di esplorare la città?
Tee vah dee es-plo-rah-reh lah chee-tah?

Would you like to have dinner with me?
Ti va di cenare con me?
Tee vah dee cheh-nah-reh kon meh?

Asking for Directions

Where is the nearest restroom?
Dove è il bagno più vicino?
Do-veh eh eel bah-nyoh pyoo vee-chee-noh?

How do I get to the train station?
Come arrivo alla stazione ferroviaria?
Koh-meh ah-ree-voh ah-lah stah-tsyoh-neh fehr-roh-vyah-ree-ah?

Can you show me on the map?
Puoi mostrarmi sulla mappa?
Pwoh-ee moh-strahr-mee sool-lah mahp-pah?

Is it far from here?
È lontano da qui?
Eh lon-tah-noh dah kwee?

Which way to the museum?
Quale strada per il museo?
Kwah-leh strah-dah pehr eel moo-seh-oh?

Where can I catch the bus?
Dove posso prendere l'autobus?
Do-veh pohs-soh prehn-deh-reh low-toh-boos?

Is this the way to the airport?
È questa la via per l'aeroporto?
Eh kwes-tah lah vee-ah pehr lah-eh-roh-por-toh?

Can you point me to the closest subway station?
Puoi indicarmi la stazione della metropolitana più vicina?
Pwoh-ee een-dee-kahr-mee lah stah-tsyoh-neh del-lah meh-troh-poh-lee-tah-nah pyoo vee-chee-nah?

I'm looking for this address.
Sto cercando questo indirizzo.
Stoh cher-kahn-doh kwes-toh een-dee-ree-tsoh.

Where is the main square?
Dove è la piazza principale?
Do-veh eh lah pyah-tzah preen-chee-pah-leh?

How far is it to the city center?
Quanto è distante il centro città?
Kwahn-toh eh dees-tahn-teh eel chen-troh chee-tah?

Can I walk there?
Posso andarci a piedi?
Pohs-soh ahn-dahr-chee ah pyeh-dee?

Do I need to take a bus?
Devo prendere un autobus?
Deh-voh prehn-deh-reh oon ow-toh-boos?

Where does this road go?
Dove porta questa strada?
Do-veh por-tah kwes-tah strah-dah?

Am I going in the right direction?
Sto andando nella giusta direzione?
Stoh ahn-dahn-doh nel-lah joo-stah dee-reh-tsyoh-neh?

Where is the closest hotel?
Dove è l'albergo più vicino?
Do-veh eh lal-behr-goh pyoo vee-chee-noh?

Can I get to the beach from here?
Posso arrivare alla spiaggia da qui?
Pohs-soh ah-ree-vah-reh ah-lah spee-ah-jjah dah kwee?

Is there a parking lot nearby?
C'è un parcheggio qui vicino?
Cheh oon par-kehj-joh kwee vee-chee-noh?

Which bus goes to the old town?
Quale autobus va alla città vecchia?
Kwah-leh ow-toh-boos vah ah-lah chee-tah vek-kya?

How to get back to this place?
Come faccio a tornare a questo posto?
Koh-meh fah-choh ah tohr-nah-reh ah kwes-toh poh-stoh?

Bank and Currency Exchange

Where can I find an ATM?
Dove posso trovare un bancomat?
Do-veh po-sso tro-va-re oon ban-ko-mat?

How do I exchange currency?
Come faccio a cambiare valuta?
Ko-meh fah-cho a kam-bya-re va-loo-tah?

What is the exchange rate today?
Qual è il tasso di cambio oggi?
Kwal eh eel tas-so dee kam-byo ohd-jee?

Can I use my credit card here?
Posso usare la mia carta di credito qui?
Po-sso oo-sa-re lah me-ah kar-tah dee kre-dee-toh kwee?

Are there any transaction fees?
Ci sono delle commissioni di transazione?
Chee so-no del-le kom-mi-ssyo-nee dee tran-sa-tsyoh-neh?

Where can I exchange foreign currency?
Dove posso cambiare valuta estera?
Do-veh po-sso kam-bya-re va-loo-tah e-ste-rah?

Do you need my passport for the exchange?
Serve il mio passaporto per il cambio?
Ser-veh eel me-oh pas-sa-por-toh per eel kam-byo?

What is the maximum amount I can withdraw?
Qual è l'importo massimo che posso prelevare?
Kwal eh leem-por-toh mas-see-moh keh po-sso preh-le-va-re?

Is there a bank nearby?
C'è una banca nelle vicinanze?
Cheh oo-nah ban-kah nel-le vee-chee-nan-tse?

Can I get change for this bill?
Posso avere il resto per questa banconota?
Po-sso a-ve-re eel re-sto per kwes-tah ban-ko-no-tah?

How much is the fee for using an ATM abroad?
Quanto è la commissione per usare un bancomat all'estero?
Kwan-toh eh lah kom-mi-ssyo-neh per oo-sa-re oon ban-ko-mat al-le-ste-roh?

Can I deposit money into my account here?
Posso depositare denaro nel mio conto qui?
Po-sso de-po-zi-ta-re deh-nah-roh nel me-oh kon-toh kwee?

What are the banking hours?
Quali sono gli orari bancari?
Kwa-lee so-no lyee oh-rah-ree ban-ka-ree?

Can I open a bank account as a tourist?
Posso aprire un conto bancario come turista?
Po-sso a-pree-re oon kon-toh ban-ka-ryo ko-meh too-ree-stah?

How can I transfer money internationally?
Come posso trasferire denaro all'estero?
Ko-meh po-sso tras-fe-ree-re deh-nah-roh al-le-ste-roh?

Is it better to exchange money at the bank or currency exchange?
È meglio cambiare denaro in banca o al cambio valuta?
Eh me-lyoh kam-bya-re deh-nah-roh een ban-kah oh al kam-byo va-loo-tah?

What documents do I need for currency exchange?
Quali documenti mi servono per il cambio valuta?
Kwa-lee do-koo-men-tee mee ser-vo-no per eel kam-byo va-loo-tah?

Can I withdraw money in local currency?
Posso prelevare denaro in valuta locale?
Po-sso preh-le-va-re deh-nah-roh een va-loo-tah lo-ka-le?

How do I find the best exchange rates?
Come faccio a trovare i migliori tassi di cambio?
Ko-meh fah-cho a tro-va-re ee myee-go-ree tas-see dee kam-byo?

Are there limits on how much currency I can bring into the country?
Ci sono limiti su quanto denaro posso portare nel paese?
Chee so-no lee-mee-tee soo kwan-to deh-nah-roh po-sso por-ta-re nel pah-e-se?

Barber

Where is the nearest barber?
Dove è il barbiere più vicino?
Wehr iz thuh nee-ruhst bahr-buhr?

Do I need an appointment for a haircut?
Ho bisogno di un appuntamento per un taglio di capelli?
Doo ahy need uhn uh-poynt-muhnt fohr uhn hae-kuht?

How much does a haircut cost?
Quanto costa un taglio di capelli?
How muhch duhz uhn hae-kuht kohst?

Can I get a shave here?
Posso farmi la barba qui?
Kahn ahy get uhn sheyv heer?

Do you offer beard trimming?
Offrite la rifinitura della barba?
Doo yoo oh-fuhr beerd trih-ming?

How long will the haircut take?
Quanto tempo ci vuole per il taglio di capelli?
How long wihl thuh hae-kuht teyk?

Can you do this hairstyle? (showing a picture)
Puoi fare questo stile di capelli? (mostrando una foto)
Kahn yoo doo thees hae-stayl? (show-ing uhn peek-chuhr)

What hair products do you use?
Quali prodotti per capelli usate?
Wuht hae proh-duhkts doo yoo yooz?

Do you have experience with curly hair?
Hai esperienza con i capelli ricci?
Doo yoo hav ek-speer-ee-uhns with kur-lee hae?

Can you recommend a hairstyle for me?
Puoi consigliarmi uno stile di capelli?
Kahn yoo rek-uh-mend uhn hae-stayl fohr mee?

What's the best way to maintain this haircut?
Qual è il modo migliore per mantenere questo taglio di capelli?
Wuhts thuh best wey tuh mayn-teyn thees hae-kuht?

Do you sell hair products here?
Vendete prodotti per capelli qui?
Doo yoo sell hae proh-duhkts heer?

Is there a discount for first-time customers?
C'è uno sconto per i clienti alla prima visita?
Iz thehr uhn dih-skownt fohr furst-taym kus-tuh-muhrz?

How busy are you today?
Quanto siete occupati oggi?
How buh-zee ahr yoo tuh-dey?

Can I choose my barber?
Posso scegliere il mio barbiere?
Kahn ahy chooz my bahr-buhr?

Do you offer hair coloring services?
Offrite servizi di colorazione dei capelli?
Doo yoo oh-fuhr hae kuhl-uhr-ing suhr-vuhs-ez?

What time do you close?
A che ora chiudete?
Wuht taym doo yoo klohz?

Do I need to wash my hair before coming?

Devo lavare i capelli prima di venire?

Doo ahy need tuh wosh my hae bee-fohr kuhm-ing?

Can you fix a bad haircut?

Puoi sistemare un taglio di capelli fatto male?

Kahn yoo fiks uhn bad hae-kuht?

Are you open on weekends?

Siete aperti nei fine settimana?

Ahr yoo oh-puhn on wee-kuhnds?

Bicycle

Where can I rent a bike?
Dove posso noleggiare una bici?
Do-veh pos-so no-le-ggia-re oo-na bee-chee?

How much does it cost to rent a bike for a day?
Quanto costa noleggiare una bici per un giorno?
Kwan-toh kos-ta no-le-ggia-re oo-na bee-chee per oon jor-no?

Is there a bike path nearby?
C'è una pista ciclabile nelle vicinanze?
Che oo-na pees-ta chee-cla-bee-le nel-le vee-chee-nan-tse?

Do I need to wear a helmet?
Devo indossare un casco?
Deh-vo in-dos-sa-re oon kas-ko?

Can I park my bike here?
Posso parcheggiare la mia bici qui?
Pos-so par-keg-gia-re la mee-a bee-chee kwee?

Are there guided bike tours?
Ci sono tour guidati in bici?
Chee so-no toor gwee-da-tee in bee-chee?

How do I lock the bike?
Come faccio a chiudere la bici con il lucchetto?
Ko-me fat-cho a kwee-de-re la bee-chee kon eel look-ket-to?

What should I do if my bike gets stolen?
Cosa devo fare se la mia bici viene rubata?
Ko-sa deh-vo fa-re se la mee-a bee-chee vyeh-ne roo-ba-ta?

Can I bring the bike on public transport?
Posso portare la bici sui mezzi pubblici?
Pos-so por-ta-re la bee-chee swee met-see poob-blee-chee?

Is it safe to cycle at night?
È sicuro andare in bici di notte?
Eh see-koo-ro an-da-re in bee-chee dee not-te?

Where can I find a bike repair shop?
Dove posso trovare un negozio di riparazione bici?
Do-veh pos-so tro-va-re oon neh-go-tso dee ree-pa-ra-tsee-o-neh bee-chee?

Do you have maps for bike routes?
Avete mappe per percorsi ciclabili?
A-veh-te map-pe per per-kor-see chee-cla-bee-lee?

Can I rent an electric bike?
Posso noleggiare una bici elettrica?
Pos-so no-le-ggia-re oo-na bee-chee e-let-tree-ka?

Are there any bike lanes in the city?
Ci sono piste ciclabili in città?
Chee so-no pees-te chee-cla-bee-lee in chee-tah?

How can I avoid theft?
Come posso evitare i furti?
Ko-me pos-so eh-vee-ta-re ee foor-tee?

What is the penalty for not locking the bike?
Qual è la penalità per non chiudere la bici con il lucchetto?
Kwal eh la peh-na-lee-tah per non kwee-de-re la bee-chee kon eel look-ket-to?

Do I need to book in advance to rent a bike?
Devo prenotare in anticipo per noleggiare una bici?
Deh-vo pre-no-ta-re in an-tee-chee-po per no-le-ggia-re oo-na bee-chee?

Can I get a discount for a long-term rental?
Posso avere uno sconto per un noleggio a lungo termine?
Pos-so a-veh-re oo-no skon-to per oon no-le-ggio a loon-go ter-mee-neh?

Where should I return the bike?
Dove devo restituire la bici?
Do-veh deh-vo res-too-e-re la bee-chee?

Is biking allowed in the park?
È permesso andare in bici nel parco?
Eh per-mes-so an-da-re in bee-chee nel par-ko?

Breakfast in Hotel

What time is breakfast served?
Dove viene servita la colazione?
Do-veh vee-eh-neh sehr-vee-tah lah ko-lah-tsyoh-neh?

Can I have breakfast in my room?
Posso avere la colazione in camera?
Pohs-soh ah-veh-reh lah ko-lah-tsyoh-neh een kah-meh-rah?

Do you have gluten-free options?
Avete opzioni senza glutine?
Ah-veh-teh ohp-tsyoh-nee sehn-zah gloo-tee-neh?

Is the breakfast buffet included in the price?
La colazione a buffet è inclusa nel prezzo?
Lah ko-lah-tsyoh-neh ah boo-f-feht eh een-kloo-sah nehl preht-tsoh?

Where can I find the breakfast room?
Dove posso trovare la sala colazioni?
Do-veh pohs-soh troh-vah-reh lah sah-lah ko-lah-tsyoh-nee?

Can I get a coffee to go?
Posso avere un caffè da portare via?
Pohs-soh ah-veh-reh oon kahf-feh dah por-tah-reh vee-ah?

Do you serve organic breakfast options?
Servite opzioni per la colazione biologica?
Sehr-vee-teh ohp-tsyoh-nee pehr lah ko-lah-tsyoh-neh bee-oh-loh-jee-kah?

What kind of milk do you have?
Che tipo di latte avete?
Keh tee-poh dee laht-teh ah-veh-teh?

Can you make a vegetarian breakfast?
Potete fare una colazione vegetariana?
Poh-teh-teh fah-reh oon-ah ko-lah-tsyoh-neh veh-jeh-tah-ree-ah-nah?

Is it possible to have breakfast earlier?
È possibile avere la colazione più presto?
Eh pohs-see-bee-leh ah-veh-reh lah ko-lah-tsyoh-neh pyoo preh-stoh?

How much does breakfast cost?
Quanto costa la colazione?
Kwahn-toh koh-stah lah ko-lah-tsyoh-neh?

Do you have vegan breakfast options?
Avete opzioni per la colazione vegana?
Ah-veh-teh ohp-tsyoh-nee pehr lah ko-lah-tsyoh-neh veh-gah-nah?

Can I invite a guest for breakfast?
Posso invitare un ospite a colazione?
Pohs-soh een-vee-tah-reh oon oh-spee-teh ah ko-lah-tsyoh-neh?

Do you have any sugar-free options?
Avete opzioni senza zucchero?
Ah-veh-teh ohp-tsyoh-nee sehn-zah zook-keh-roh?

Can I order room service for breakfast?
Posso ordinare il servizio in camera per la colazione?
Pohs-soh or-dee-nah-reh eel sehr-vee-tsyoh een kah-meh-rah pehr lah ko-lah-tsyoh-neh?

What types of bread do you offer?
Quali tipi di pane offrite?
Kwah-lee tee-pee dee pah-neh ohf-free-teh?

Is there a dress code for breakfast?
C'è un codice di abbigliamento per la colazione?
Cheh oon koh-dee-cheh dee ab-bee-glyah-men-toh pehr lah ko-lah-tsyoh-neh?

How long is breakfast served?
Per quanto tempo viene servita la colazione?
Pehr kwahn-toh tem-poh vee-eh-neh sehr-vee-tah lah ko-lah-tsyoh-neh?

Do you have lactose-free milk?
Avete latte senza lattosio?
Ah-veh-teh laht-teh sehn-zah laht-toh-syoh?

Can I have eggs made to order?
Posso avere uova su ordinazione?
Pohs-soh ah-veh-reh woh-vah soo or-dee-nah-tsyoh-neh?

Bus Stop

Where is the nearest bus stop?
Dove è la fermata dell'autobus più vicina?
Doh-veh eh lah fehr-mah-tah del-l'ow-toh-boos pee-oo vee-chee-nah?

Which bus goes to the city center?
Quale autobus va al centro città?
Kwah-leh ow-toh-boos vah ahl chen-troh chee-tah?

What time is the first bus in the morning?
A che ora passa il primo autobus la mattina?
Ah keh oh-rah pah-sah eel pree-moh ow-toh-boos lah maht-tee-nah?

How much is the bus fare?
Quanto costa il biglietto dell'autobus?
Kwahn-toh koh-stah eel bee-lyet-toh del-l'ow-toh-boos?

Can I buy a bus ticket here?
Posso comprare qui un biglietto dell'autobus?
Pohs-soh kom-prah-reh kwee oon bee-lyet-toh del-l'ow-toh-boos?

Does this bus go to the airport?
Questo autobus va all'aeroporto?
Kwes-toh ow-toh-boos vah ahl-l'ah-eh-roh-por-toh?

How often do buses run to the city center?
Ogni quanto passano gli autobus per il centro città?
Oh-nyee kwahn-toh pah-sah-noh lyee ow-toh-boos pehr eel chen-troh chee-tah?

Is this the right stop for the museum?
È questa la fermata giusta per il museo?
Eh kwes-tah lah fehr-mah-tah joo-stah pehr eel moo-zeh-oh?

What time does the last bus leave?
A che ora parte l'ultimo autobus?
Ah keh oh-rah pahr-teh l'ool-tee-moh ow-toh-boos?

Can you tell me when to get off to reach train station?
Puoi dirmi quando scendere per la stazione ferroviaria?
Pwoh-ee deer-mee kwahn-doh shen-deh-reh pehr lah stah-tsyoh-neh fehr-roh-vee-ah-ree-ah?

Where do I buy a bus pass?
Dove posso comprare un abbonamento per l'autobus?
Doh-veh pohs-soh kom-prah-reh oon ahb-boh-nah-men-toh pehr l'ow-toh-boos?

Does this bus stop at the hospital?
Questo autobus ferma all'ospedale?
Kwes-toh ow-toh-boos fehr-mah ahl-loh-speh-dah-leh?

Are pets allowed on the bus?
Gli animali sono ammessi sull'autobus?
Lyee ah-nee-mah-lee soh-noh ahm-mes-see sool-l'ow-toh-boos?

How do I signal to get off the bus?
Come faccio a segnalare per scendere dall'autobus?
Koh-meh fah-choh ah seh-nyah-lah-reh pehr shen-deh-reh dal-l'ow-toh-boos?

Is there a day pass for the bus?
C'è un biglietto giornaliero per l'autobus?
Cheh oon bee-lyet-toh johr-nah-lee-eh-roh pehr l'ow-toh-boos?

Can I use my bus ticket more than once?
Posso usare il mio biglietto dell'autobus più di una volta?
Pohs-soh oo-zah-reh eel mee-oh bee-lyet-toh del-l'ow-toh-boos pyoo dee oo-nah vol-tah?

What's the schedule for the bus on weekends?
Qual è l'orario degli autobus nei fine settimana?
Kwah-leh loh-rah-ree-oh deh-lyee ow-toh-boos nay feen-eh set-tee-mah-nah?

Do I need an exact change for the bus fare?
Serve il resto esatto per il biglietto dell'autobus?
Sehr-veh eel res-toh ehz-zahk-toh pehr eel bee-lyet-toh del-l'ow-toh-boos?

Where can I find the bus route map?
Dove posso trovare la mappa del percorso dell'autobus?
Doh-veh pohs-soh troh-vah-reh lah mahp-pah del pehr-kor-soh del-l'ow-toh-boos?

Is there a direct bus to the beach?
C'è un autobus diretto per la spiaggia?
Cheh oon ow-toh-boos dee-ret-toh pehr lah spee-ahj-jah?

Buying a SIM Card

Do you sell SIM cards?
Vendete SIM?
Ven-deh-teh SEEM?

How much is a SIM card?
Quanto costa una SIM?
Kwahn-toh koh-stah oo-nah SEEM?

Can I buy a prepaid SIM card here?
Posso comprare una SIM prepagata qui?
Pohs-soh kom-prah-reh oo-nah SEEM preh-pah-gah-tah kwee?

Do I need my passport to buy a SIM card?
Ho bisogno del mio passaporto per comprare una SIM?
Oh bee-zoh-nyoh del mee-oh pahs-sah-por-toh pehr kom-prah-reh oo-nah SEEM?

Which mobile operator do you recommend?
Quale operatore mobile consigliate?
Kwah-leh oh-peh-rah-toh-reh moh-bee-leh kon-see-lyah-teh?

Does this SIM card work internationally?
Questa SIM funziona all'estero?
Kwes-tah SEEM foon-tsyoh-nah ahl-leh-steh-roh?

How long does the SIM card activation take?
Quanto tempo ci vuole per l'attivazione della SIM?
Kwahn-toh tem-poh chee vwo-leh pehr laht-tee-vah-tsyoh-neh del-lah SEEM?

Can I top up my SIM card here?
Posso ricaricare la mia SIM qui?
Pohs-soh ree-kah-ree-kah-reh lah mee-ah SEEM kwee?

What are the data plans for this SIM card?
Quali sono i piani dati per questa SIM?
*Kwah-lee soh-noh ee pyah-nee dah-tee pehr kwes-tah
SEEM?*

Is there a package for tourists?
C'è un pacchetto per turisti?
Cheh oon pahk-keh-toh pehr too-ree-stee?

How do I check the balance of my SIM card?
Come faccio a controllare il saldo della mia SIM?
*Koh-meh fah-tchoh ah kon-trohl-lah-reh eel sahl-doh del-lah
mee-ah SEEM?*

Can I use this SIM in multiple countries?
Posso usare questa SIM in più paesi?
Pohs-soh oo-zah-reh kwes-tah SEEM een pyoo pah-eh-zee?

Do you have any special offers for SIM cards?
Avete offerte speciali per le SIM?
Ah-veh-teh oh-fehr-teh speh-chah-lee pehr leh SEEM?

What is the validity period of this SIM card?
Qual è il periodo di validità di questa SIM?
*Kwah-leh eel peh-ree-oh-doh dee vah-lee-dee-tah dee kwes-
tah SEEM?*

Can I get a SIM card with unlimited data?
Posso avere una SIM con dati illimitati?
Pohs-soh ah-veh-reh oo-nah SEEM kon dah-tee eel-lee-mee-tah-tee?

How can I activate international roaming on this SIM?
Come posso attivare il roaming internazionale su questa SIM?
Koh-meh pohs-soh ah-tee-vah-reh eel roh-ming een-tehr-nah-tsyoh-nah-leh soo kwes-tah SEEM?

Do I need to configure my phone to use this SIM?
Devo configurare il mio telefono per usare questa SIM?
Deh-voh kon-fee-goo-rah-reh eel mee-oh teh-leh-foh-noh pehr oo-zah-reh kwes-tah SEEM?

What documents do I need to buy a SIM card?
Quali documenti mi servono per comprare una SIM?
Kwah-lee doh-koo-men-tee mee sehr-voh-noh pehr kom-prah-reh oo-nah SEEM?

Can I choose my phone number?
Posso scegliere il mio numero di telefono?
Pohs-soh sheh-lyeh-reh eel mee-oh noo-meh-roh dee teh-leh-foh-noh?

Is it possible to buy a SIM card online?
È possibile comprare una SIM online?
Eh pohs-see-bee-leh kom-prah-reh oo-nah SEEM ohn-line?

Camping

Where is the nearest camping site?
Dove è il campeggio più vicino?
Do-veh eh eel kam-pej-joh pyoo vee-chee-noh?

Can I rent a tent here?
Posso affittare una tenda qui?
Pohs-soh ahf-fee-tah-reh oo-nah ten-dah kwee?

Is there a source of drinking water?
C'è una fonte di acqua potabile?
Cheh oo-nah fon-teh dee ahk-wah poh-tah-bee-leh?

Where can I dispose of trash?
Dove posso smaltire i rifiuti?
Do-veh pohs-soh smahl-tee-reh ee ree-foo-tee?

Can I light a fire here?
Posso accendere un fuoco qui?
Pohs-soh ah-chen-deh-reh oon fwoh-koh kwee?

Do you have a map of the trails?
Avete una mappa dei sentieri?
Ah-veh-teh oo-nah mahp-pah dey sen-tyeh-ree?

Where are the showers?
Dove sono le docce?
Do-veh soh-noh leh doh-cheh?

Can I park my car here?
Posso parcheggiare la mia auto qui?
Pohs-soh par-keh-jah-reh lah mee-ah ow-toh kwee?

How much is the camping fee?
Quanto costa la tariffa del campeggio?
Kwahn-toh koh-stah lah tah-ree-fah del kam-pej-joh?

Is there a quiet time?
C'è un orario di silenzio?
Cheh oon oh-rah-ree-oh dee see-len-tsyoh?

Where can I charge my phone?
Dove posso caricare il mio telefono?
Do-veh pohs-soh kah-ree-kah-reh eel mee-oh teh-leh-foh-noh?

Do you rent bicycles?
Affittate biciclette?
Ahf-fee-tah-teh bee-chee-klet-teh?

Can I bring my dog?
Posso portare il mio cane?
Pohs-soh pohr-tah-reh eel mee-oh kah-neh?

Are there any dangerous animals?
Ci sono animali pericolosi?
Chee soh-noh ah-nee-mah-lee peh-ree-koh-loh-see?

Where can I buy firewood?
Dove posso comprare la legna da fuoco?
Do-veh pohs-soh kom-prah-reh lah leh-nyah dah fwoh-koh?

Can I fish in the lake?
Posso pescare nel lago?
Pohs-soh peh-skah-reh nel lah-goh?

Do you have a first aid kit?
Avete un kit di primo soccorso?
Ah-veh-teh oon keet dee pree-moh soh-kohr-soh?

Is it safe to swim here?
È sicuro nuotare qui?
Eh see-koo-roh nwah-tah-reh kwee?

Can you recommend hiking routes?
Puoi consigliare percorsi di escursionismo?
Pwoh-ee kon-see-lyah-reh pehr-kor-see dee eh-skur-syoh-nee-smoh?

Where is the closest emergency facility?
Dove è la struttura di emergenza più vicina?
Do-veh eh lah strutt-oo-rah dee eh-mehr-jen-tsah pyoo vee-chee-nah?

Celiac Disease - Gluten Free

Do you have gluten-free options?
Avete opzioni senza glutine?
Ah-veh-teh op-tsyoh-nee sehn-zah gloo-tee-neh?

Is this dish gluten-free?
Questo piatto è senza glutine?
Kweh-stoh pyah-toh eh sehn-zah gloo-tee-neh?

Can you prepare gluten-free meals?
Potete preparare pasti senza glutine?
Poh-teh-teh preh-pah-rah-reh pah-stee sehn-zah gloo-tee-neh?

Do you use separate cooking utensils for gluten-free food?
Usate utensili da cucina separati per il cibo senza glutine?
Oo-zah-teh oo-ten-see-lee dah koo-chee-nah sehp-ah-rah-tee per eel chee-boh sehn-zah gloo-tee-neh?

Can I see the gluten-free menu?
Posso vedere il menù senza glutine?
Pohs-soh veh-deh-reh eel meh-noo sehn-zah gloo-tee-neh?

Is the bread gluten-free?
Il pane è senza glutine?
Eel pah-neh eh sehn-zah gloo-tee-neh?

Do you have gluten-free pasta?
Avete pasta senza glutine?
Ah-veh-teh pah-stah sehn-zah gloo-tee-neh?

Are your sauces gluten-free?
Le vostre salse sono senza glutine?
Leh voh-streh sahl-seh soh-noh sehn-zah gloo-tee-neh?

Can you make a gluten-free pizza?
Potete fare una pizza senza glutine?
Poh-teh-teh fah-reh oo-nah peet-zah sehn-zah gloo-tee-neh?

Do you have any gluten-free desserts?
Avete dei dolci senza glutine?
Ah-veh-teh deh-ee dohl-chee sehn-zah gloo-tee-neh?

Is there gluten in this sauce?
C'è glutine in questa salsa?
Cheh gloo-tee-neh een kweh-stah sahl-sah?

How is your gluten-free food prepared?
Come viene preparato il vostro cibo senza glutine?
Koh-meh vyeh-neh preh-pah-rah-toh eel voh-stroh chee-boh sehn-zah gloo-tee-neh?

Do you have a separate gluten-free cooking area?
Avete un'area di cottura separata per il cibo senza glutine?
Ah-veh-teh oon-ah-eh-reh-ah dee koh-too-rah sehp-ah-rah-tah per eel chee-boh sehn-zah gloo-tee-neh?

Can I have a gluten-free beer?
Posso avere una birra senza glutine?
Pohs-soh ah-veh-reh oo-nah beer-rah sehn-zah gloo-tee-neh?

Are the fries cooked in the same oil as gluten-containing dishes?
Le patatine sono fritte nello stesso olio dei piatti con glutine?
Leh pah-tah-tee-neh soh-noh free-teh nehl-loh stehs-soh oh-lee-oh deh-ee pyah-tee kohn gloo-tee-neh?

Can you recommend a gluten-free dish?
Potete consigliare un piatto senza glutine?
Poh-teh-teh kohn-see-lyah-reh oon pyah-toh sehn-zah gloo-tee-neh?

Do you have gluten-free breakfast options?
Avete opzioni per la colazione senza glutine?
Ah-veh-teh op-tsyoh-nee pehr lah koh-lah-tsyoh-neh sehn-zah gloo-tee-neh?

Is the soup gluten-free?
La zuppa è senza glutine?
Lah tsoop-pah eh sehn-zah gloo-tee-neh?

Can you avoid cross-contamination with gluten?
Potete evitare la contaminazione incrociata con il glutine?
Poh-teh-teh eh-vee-tah-reh lah kohn-tah-mee-nah-tsyoh-neh een-kroh-chah-tah kohn eel gloo-tee-neh?

Do you offer gluten-free snacks?
Offrite snack senza glutine?
Ohf-free-teh snahk sehn-zah gloo-tee-neh?

Cigarettes

Is smoking allowed here?
Dove è permesso fumare?
Do-veh eh per-mes-so foo-ma-re?

Where can I buy cigarettes?
Dove posso comprare sigarette?
Do-veh pos-so com-pra-re see-ga-ret-te?

Do you sell electronic cigarettes?
Vendete sigarette elettroniche?
Ven-de-te see-ga-ret-te e-let-tro-ni-che?

Can I smoke inside?
Posso fumare all'interno?
Pos-so foo-ma-re al-lin-ter-no?

What brands of cigarettes do you have?
Quali marche di sigarette avete?
Kwa-li mar-che di see-ga-ret-te a-ve-te?

Is there a smoking area nearby?
C'è un'area fumatori nelle vicinanze?
Che oon a-rea foo-ma-to-ri nel-le vi-ci-nan-ze?

How much is a pack of cigarettes?
Quanto costa un pacchetto di sigarette?
Kwan-to cos-ta oon pak-ket-to di see-ga-ret-te?

Do I need an ID to buy cigarettes?
Serve un documento per comprare sigarette?
Ser-ve oon do-cu-men-to per com-pra-re see-ga-ret-te?

Are vaping products available here?
I prodotti per svapare sono disponibili qui?
Ee pro-dot-ti per sva-pa-re so-no di-spo-ni-bi-li kwee?

Can I smoke on the balcony?
Posso fumare sul balcone?
Pos-so foo-ma-re sool bal-co-ne?

Where is the closest tobacco shop?
Dove è il tabaccaio più vicino?
Do-veh eh eel ta-bak-kajo pyoo vee-chee-no?

Do you have lighters?
Avete accendini?
A-ve-te ac-cen-di-ni?

Can I try this vape flavor?
Posso provare questo aroma per sigaretta elettronica?
Pos-so pro-va-re kwes-to a-ro-ma per see-ga-ret-ta e-let-tro-ni-ca?

What is the smoking policy here?
Qual è la politica sul fumo qui?
Kwal eh la po-lee-tee-ca sool foo-mo kwee?

Are there any smoking rooms?
Ci sono stanze per fumatori?
Che so-no stan-tze per foo-ma-to-ri?

Do you sell tobacco for rolling cigarettes?
Vendete tabacco da rollare?
Ven-de-te ta-bak-ko da rol-la-re?

Is it legal to smoke in public places?
È legale fumare in luoghi pubblici?
Eh le-ga-le foo-ma-re in loo-ghee pub-bli-ci?
46

Can I have a matchbox?
Posso avere una scatola di fiammiferi?
Pos-so a-ve-re oona ska-to-la di fjam-mi-fe-ri?

Where can I dispose of cigarette butts?
Dove posso buttare i mozziconi di sigaretta?
Do-veh pos-so but-ta-re ee mot-tsee-co-nee di see-ga-ret-ta?

Do you have menthol cigarettes?
Avete sigarette al mentolo?
A-ve-te see-ga-ret-te al men-to-lo?

Coffee Shop

Can I have a coffee, please?
Posso avere un caffè, per favore?
Pohs-soh ah-veh-reh oon kahf-feh, pehr fah-voh-reh?

What kinds of coffee do you have?
Quali tipi di caffè avete?
Kwah-lee tee-pee dee kahf-feh ah-veh-teh?

Do you have almond milk?
Avete latte di mandorla?
Ah-veh-teh laht-teh dee man-dohr-lah?

Could I get a slice of cake?
Potrei avere una fetta di torta?
Poh-treh-ee ah-veh-reh oo-nah feht-tah dee tohr-tah?

Is this gluten-free?
Questo è senza glutine?
Kwes-toh eh sehn-zah gloo-tee-neh?

How much is a cappuccino?
Quanto costa un cappuccino?
Kwahn-toh kohs-tah oon kahp-poo-chee-noh?

Can I pay by card?
Posso pagare con la carta?
Pohs-soh pah-gah-reh kohn lah kahr-tah?

Do you have Wi-Fi here?
Avete Wi-Fi qui?
Ah-veh-teh wee-fee kwee?

Can I have the bill, please?
Posso avere il conto, per favore?
Pohs-soh ah-veh-reh eel kohn-toh, pehr fah-voh-reh?

Do you have any vegan options?
Avete opzioni vegane?
Ah-veh-teh ohp-tsyoh-nee veh-gah-neh?

Is the coffee fair trade?
Il caffè è equo commercio?
Eel kahf-feh eh eh-kwoh koh-mehr-tsyoh?

Can I get it to go?
Posso averlo da portare via?
Pohs-soh ah-vehr-loh dah pohr-tah-reh vee-ah?

Do you have soy milk?
Avete latte di soia?
Ah-veh-teh laht-teh dee soy-ah?

What's the Wi-Fi password?
Qual è la password del Wi-Fi?
Kwah-leh lah pahs-wuhrd dehl wee-fee?

Can I sit here?
Posso sedermi qui?
Pohs-soh seh-dehr-mee kwee?

Do you offer any discounts?
Offrite sconti?
Ohf-free-teh skohn-tee?

Could you heat it up, please?
Potreste scaldarlo, per favore?
Poh-tres-teh skahl-dahr-loh, pehr fah-voh-reh?

What's the special today?

Qual è lo speciale di oggi?

Kwah-leh loh speh-chah-leh dee ohd-jee?

Is there a table available?

C'è un tavolo disponibile?

Cheh oon tah-voh-loh dee-spoh-nee-bee-leh?

Can I see the menu, please?

Potrei vedere il menù, per favore?

Poh-treh-ee veh-deh-reh eel meh-noo, pehr fah-voh-reh?

Computers and Internet

Do you have Wi-Fi?
Avete Wi-Fi?
Ah-veh-teh Wee-Fee?

What's the Wi-Fi password?
Qual è la password del Wi-Fi?
Kwah-l eh lah pahs-wuhrd del Wee-Fee?

Is the internet connection fast?
La connessione internet è veloce?
Lah koh-nneh-syoh-neh een-tehr-net eh veh-loh-cheh?

How do I connect to the Wi-Fi?
Come mi collego al Wi-Fi?
Koh-meh mee kohl-leh-goh ahl Wee-Fee?

Can I use the computer?
Posso usare il computer?
Pohs-soh oo-zah-reh eel kohm-pyoo-tehr?

I need to check my email.
Devo controllare la mia email.
Deh-voh kohn-trohl-lah-reh lah mee-ah ee-mehl.

Where can I print documents?
Dove posso stampare documenti?
Doh-veh pohs-soh stahm-pah-reh doh-koo-mehn-tee?

Do you have a scanner?
Avete uno scanner?
Ah-veh-teh oo-noh skah-nner?

I need to download a file.
Devo scaricare un file.
Deh-voh skah-ree-kah-reh oon fee-leh.

How do I upload photos?
Come faccio a caricare foto?
Koh-meh fah-choh ah kah-ree-kah-reh foh-toh?

Is there a charge for using the internet?
C'è un costo per usare internet?
Cheh oon kohs-toh pehr oo-zah-reh een-tehr-net?

Can I have access to a cloud service?
Posso avere accesso a un servizio cloud?
Pohs-soh ah-veh-reh ahk-chess-soh ah oon sehr-vee-tsyoh klowd?

I need to update my software.
Devo aggiornare il mio software.
Deh-voh ahj-johr-nah-reh eel mee-oh sohf-twah-reh.

How can I protect my privacy online?
Come posso proteggere la mia privacy online?
Koh-meh pohs-soh proh-teh-jeh-reh lah mee-ah pree-vah-see ohn-line?

Do you have an Ethernet cable?
Avete un cavo Ethernet?
Ah-veh-teh oon kah-voh Eh-thehr-net?

I need to reboot the computer.
Devo riavviare il computer.
Deh-voh ree-ahv-vyah-reh eel kohm-pyoo-tehr.

Where can I find free Wi-Fi?
Dove posso trovare Wi-Fi gratuito?

Doh-veh pohs-soh troh-vah-reh Wee-Fee grah-too-ee-toh?

Can I have a USB drive?
Posso avere una chiavetta USB?
Pohs-soh ah-veh-reh oo-nah kyah-veh-tah Oo-Ess-Bee?

Is it safe to use public Wi-Fi?
È sicuro usare il Wi-Fi pubblico?
Eh see-koo-roh oo-zah-reh eel Wee-Fee poob-blee-koh?

How do I find a tech support service?
Come trovo un servizio di assistenza tecnica?
Koh-meh troh-voh oon sehr-vee-tsyoh dee ah-sees-ten-tsah teh-knee-kah?

Dairy-Free

I am lactose intolerant.
Sono intollerante al lattosio.
So-no een-toh-leh-rahn-teh ahl laht-toh-syoh.

Does this dish contain lactose?
Questo piatto contiene lattosio?
Kwest-oh pyah-toh kohn-tyeh-neh laht-toh-syoh?

I cannot have dairy products.
Non posso mangiare latticini.
Non pohs-soh mahn-jah-reh laht-tee-chee-nee.

Is there any milk in this?
C'è latte in questo?
Cheh laht-teh een kwest-oh?

Can you prepare it without dairy?
Può prepararlo senza latticini?
Pwoh preh-pah-rahr-loh sen-tsah laht-tee-chee-nee?

I am allergic to lactose.
Sono allergico al lattosio.
So-no ahl-ler-jee-koh ahl laht-toh-syoh.

I need a lactose-free menu.
Ho bisogno di un menù senza lattosio.
Oh bee-zoh-nyoh dee oon meh-noo sen-tsah laht-toh-syoh.

Can I have a lactose-free version?
Posso avere una versione senza lattosio?
Pohs-soh ah-veh-reh oo-nah vehr-syoh-neh sen-tsah laht-toh-syoh?

Are there any lactose-free options?
Ci sono opzioni senza lattosio?
Chee so-no op-tsyoh-nee sen-tsah laht-toh-syoh?

This is for someone with a lactose allergy.
Questo è per qualcuno con un'allergia al lattosio.
*Kwest-oh eh pehr kwahl-koo-noh kohn oon ahl-ler-jee-ah ahl
laht-toh-syoh.*

Can you recommend a lactose-free dish?
Può consigliare un piatto senza lattosio?
Pwoh kohn-see-lyah-reh oon pyah-toh sen-tsah laht-toh-syoh?

I can't drink milk.
Non posso bere latte.
Non pohs-soh beh-reh laht-teh.

Does this sauce contain cream?
Questa salsa contiene panna?
Kwest-ah sahl-sah kohn-tyeh-neh pahn-nah?

Is this cheese lactose-free?
Questo formaggio è senza lattosio?
Kwest-oh for-maj-joh eh sen-tsah laht-toh-syoh?

Please, no butter.
Per favore, niente burro.
Pehr fah-voh-reh, nyen-teh boor-roh.

Is the bread made with milk?
Il pane è fatto con latte?
Eel pah-neh eh faht-toh kohn laht-teh?

Can you make it without cheese?
Può farlo senza formaggio?

Pwoh fahr-loh sen-tsah for-maj-joh?

Does this dessert have dairy?

Questo dolce contiene latticini?

Kwest-oh dohl-cheh kohn-tyeh-neh laht-tee-chee-nee?

Is there any yogurt in this?

C'è yogurt in questo?

Cheh yo-goort een kwest-oh?

I need a dairy-free breakfast.

Ho bisogno di una colazione senza latticini.

Oh bee-zoh-nyoh dee oo-nah koh-lah-tsyoh-neh sen-tsah laht-tee-chee-nee.

Describe Your Job and Origin

I am a teacher.
Sono un insegnante.
Soh-noh oon een-sehn-yahn-teh

I work in healthcare.
Lavoro nel settore sanitario.
Lah-voh-roh nel seh-toh-reh sah-nee-tah-ree-oh

I'm an engineer.
Sono un ingegnere.
Soh-noh oon een-jeh-neh-reh

I'm a student.
Sono uno studente.
Soh-noh oo-noh stoo-dehn-teh

I work in technology.
Lavoro nella tecnologia.
Lah-voh-roh nel-lah tehk-noh-loh-jee-ah

I am a freelance writer.
Sono uno scrittore freelance.
Soh-noh oo-noh skree-toh-reh freh-lahn-cheh

I'm from a small town.
Vengo da una piccola città.
Vehn-goh dah oo-nah peek-koh-lah chee-tah

I work in finance.
Lavoro nelle finanze.
Lah-voh-roh neh-lleh fee-nahn-tseh

I am a photographer.
Sono un fotografo.

Soh-noh oon foh-toh-grah-foh

I'm originally from Japan.
Sono originario del Giappone.
Soh-noh oh-ree-jee-nah-ree-oh del Jah-poh-neh

I am a chef.
Sono uno chef.
Soh-noh oo-noh shehf

I work in marketing.
Lavoro nel marketing.
Lah-voh-roh nel mahr-keh-teen-g

I'm from a big city.
Vengo da una grande città.
Vehn-goh dah oo-nah grahn-deh chee-tah

I am a software developer.
Sono uno sviluppatore di software.
Soh-noh oo-noh svee-loo-pah-toh-reh dee sohf-twah-reh

I come from a rural area.
Vengo da una zona rurale.
Vehn-goh dah oo-nah tsoh-nah roo-rah-leh

I work for a non-profit organization.
Lavoro per un'organizzazione non profit.
Lah-voh-roh pehr oon'or-gah-nee-tsa-tsyoh-neh non proh-feet

I am an artist.
Sono un artista.
Soh-noh oon ahr-tee-stah
I'm from the coast.
Vengo dalla costa.

Vehn-goh dah-lah koh-stah

I am a business owner.
Sono il proprietario di un'azienda.
Soh-noh eel pro-pree-tah-ree-oh dee oon'ah-tsyehn-dah

I come from the United States.
Io vengo dagli Stati Uniti.
Ee-oh VEN-goh DAH-lyee STA-tee OO-nee-tee

I come from Canada.
Io vengo dal Canada.
Ee-oh VEN-goh dal Ca-na-da

I come from the United Kingdom.
Io vengo dal Regno Unito.
Ee-oh VEN-goh dal REH-gno OO-nee-toh

I come from Australia.
Io vengo dall'Australia.
Ee-oh VEN-goh dal-low-STRAH-lee-ah

I come from New Zealand.
Io vengo dalla Nuova Zelanda.
Ee-oh VEN-goh DAH-lah NWOh-vah dzeh-LAHN-dah

I come from Ireland.
Io vengo dall'Irlanda.
Ee-oh VEN-goh dal-EER-lahn-dah

Dentist

Where is the nearest dentist?
Dove è il dentista più vicino?
Do-veh eh eel den-tee-stah pyoo vee-chee-noh?

How can I book an appointment?
Come posso prenotare un appuntamento?
Ko-meh pos-so preh-no-tah-reh oon ah-poon-tah-men-toh?

I have a toothache.
Ho mal di denti.
Oh mal dee den-tee.

Is the dentist available today?
Il dentista è disponibile oggi?
Eel den-tee-stah eh dee-spo-nee-bee-leh oh-jee?

Can I pay with a credit card?
Posso pagare con una carta di credito?
Pos-so pah-gah-reh kon oo-nah car-tah dee creh-dee-toh?

Do you offer emergency services?
Offrite servizi di emergenza?
Of-free-teh ser-vee-tzee dee eh-mer-jen-zah?

How long will the treatment take?
Quanto tempo richiede il trattamento?
Kwan-toh tem-poh ree-chye-deh eel trat-tah-men-toh?

Where can I fill a prescription?
Dove posso fare la ricetta?
Do-veh pos-so fah-reh lah ree-chet-tah?

Do you have dental insurance?
Hai l'assicurazione dentale?
Eye las-see-koo-rah-tsee-oh-neh den-tah-leh?

I need an X-ray.
Ho bisogno di una radiografia.
Oh bee-so-nyoh dee oo-nah rah-dee-oh-grah-fee-ah.

Can you recommend a good dentist?
Puoi consigliare un buon dentista?
Pwoy kon-sil-yah-reh oon bwon den-tee-stah?

What are your opening hours?
Quali sono gli orari di apertura?
Kwah-lee soh-noh glee oh-rah-ree dee ah-per-too-rah?

I have an allergic reaction.
Ho una reazione allergica.
Oh oo-nah reh-ah-tsee-oh-neh al-ler-gee-kah.

Is it necessary to make an appointment?
È necessario prendere un appuntamento?
Eh neh-ches-sah-ree-oh pren-deh-reh oon ah-poon-tah-men-toh?

How much will it cost?
Quanto costerà?
Kwan-toh kos-teh-rah?

Do you do teeth whitening?
Fate lo sbiancamento dei denti?
Fah-teh loh sbee-ahn-kah-men-toh day den-tee?

What should I do if I have an emergency?
Cosa devo fare in caso di emergenza?
Koh-sah deh-voh fah-reh een kah-zoh dee eh-mer-jen-zah?

Can I see the dentist without an appointment?
Posso vedere il dentista senza appuntamento?
Pos-so veh-deh-reh eel den-tee-stah sen-zah ah-poon-tah-men-toh?

I need a dental check-up.
Ho bisogno di un controllo dentale.
Oh bee-so-nyoh dee oon kon-trol-loh den-tah-leh.

Diabetics

Do you have any sugar-free options?
Avete opzioni senza zucchero?
Ah-veh-teh op-tsyoh-nee sehn-zah tsoo-kkeh-roh?

Can I see the nutritional information?
Posso vedere le informazioni nutrizionali?
Pohs-soh veh-deh-reh leh in-for-mah-tsyoh-nee noo-tree-tsyoh-nah-lee?

Is this dish high in carbohydrates?
Questo piatto è ricco di carboidrati?
Kweh-stoh pyah-toh eh ree-kkoh dee kar-boh-ee-dra-tee?

Can I have a meal with zero carbohydrates?
Posso avere un pasto senza carboidrati?
Pohs-soh ah-veh-reh oon pah-stoh sehn-zah kar-boh-ee-dra-tee?

Where is the nearest pharmacy?
Dove è la farmacia più vicina?
Doh-veh eh lah far-mah-tsyah pyoo vee-chee-nah?

I need to check my blood sugar, can I have some privacy?
Devo controllare il mio livello di zucchero, posso avere un po' di privacy?
Deh-voh kohn-troh-lah-reh eel mee-oh lee-veh-loh dee tsoo-kkeh-roh, pohs-soh ah-veh-reh oon poh dee pree-vah-tsee?

Can you store my insulin in the fridge?
Potete conservare la mia insulina in frigo?
Poh-teh-teh kohn-ser-vah-reh lah mee-ah in-soo-lee-nah een free-goh?

I am diabetic, can I have this without sugar?
Sono diabetico, posso avere questo senza zucchero?
Soh-noh dee-ah-beh-tee-koh, pohs-soh ah-veh-reh kweh-stoh sehn-zah tsoo-kkeh-roh?

Does this contain any artificial sweeteners?
Contiene dolcificanti artificiali?
Kohn-tyeh-neh dohl-chee-fee-kahn-tee ar-tee-fee-tsyah-lee?

Can I have a list of ingredients?
Posso avere la lista degli ingredienti?
Pohs-soh ah-veh-reh lah lee-stah dehl-ee in-greh-dee-ehn-tee?

Is it possible to have a lower-fat option?
È possibile avere un'opzione a basso contenuto di grassi?
Eh poh-see-bee-leh ah-veh-reh oon-op-tsyoh-neh ah bahs-soh kohn-teh-noo-toh dee grahs-see?

Can I get a glass of water, please?
Posso avere un bicchiere d'acqua, per favore?
Pohs-soh ah-veh-reh oon bee-kkyeh-reh dah-kwah, pehr fah-voh-reh?

I need to take my medication now, is there a quiet place?
Devo prendere la mia medicina ora, c'è un posto tranquillo?
Deh-voh prehn-deh-reh lah mee-ah meh-dee-chee-nah oh-rah, cheh oon pohs-toh trahn-kweel-loh?

Can I have an extra portion of vegetables?
Posso avere una porzione extra di verdure?
Pohs-soh ah-veh-reh oo-nah pohr-tsyoh-neh ehk-strah dee vehr-doo-reh?

Do you have any meals prepared without salt?
Avete piatti preparati senza sale?
Ah-veh-teh pyah-tee preh-pah-rah-tee sehn-zah sah-leh?

Can I speak to the chef about my dietary needs?
Posso parlare con lo chef riguardo le mie esigenze
alimentari?
*Pohs-soh pahr-lah-reh kohn loh shehf ree-gwahr-doh leh
mee-eh eh-zee-jehn-tseh ah-lee-men-tah-ree?*

I am allergic to nuts, does this dish contain any?
Sono allergico alle noci, questo piatto ne contiene?
*Soh-noh al-ler-jee-koh ah-lleh noh-chee, kweh-stoh pyah-toh
neh kohn-tyeh-neh?*

Could you recommend a sugar-free dessert?
Potreste consigliarmi un dolce senza zucchero?
*Poh-trehs-teh kohn-see-lyahr-mee oon dohl-tseh sehn-zah
tsoo-kkeh-roh?*

Do you have gluten-free options as well?
Avete anche opzioni senza glutine?
Ah-veh-teh ahn-keh op-tsyoh-nee sehn-zah gloo-tee-neh?

I must avoid fried foods, what do you recommend?
Devo evitare i cibi fritti, cosa consigliate?
*Deh-voh eh-vee-tah-reh ee chee-bee free-tee, koh-sah kohn-
see-lyah-teh?*

Electronic Payments

Do you accept credit cards?
Accettate carte di credito?
Ah-chet-tah-teh kar-teh dee kre-dee-toh?

Can I pay with PayPal?
Posso pagare con PayPal?
Pohs-soh pah-gah-reh kohn Pay-Pal?

Is there a fee for card payments?
C'è una commissione per i pagamenti con carta?
Cheh oo-nah koh-mees-see-oh-neh pehr ee pah-gah-men-tee kohn kar-tah?

Where can I find an ATM?
Dove posso trovare un bancomat?
Do-veh pohs-soh troh-vah-reh oon bahn-koh-mat?

Do you accept Bitcoin?
Accettate Bitcoin?
Ah-chet-tah-teh Bee-tkoh-een?

Is it safe to use my card here?
È sicuro usare la mia carta qui?
Eh see-koo-roh oo-sah-reh lah meeah kar-tah kwee?

How much is the transaction fee?
Quanto è la commissione di transazione?
Kwahn-toh eh lah koh-mees-see-oh-neh dee trahn-sah-tsee-oh-neh?

Can I get a receipt for my payment?
Posso avere una ricevuta per il mio pagamento?
Pohs-soh ah-veh-reh oo-nah ree-cheh-voo-tah pehr eel meeo pah-gah-men-toh?

Do you offer cashback with purchases?
Offrite cashback con gli acquisti?
Ohf-free-teh kahsh-bahk kohn glee ahk-kwees-tee?

How do I use contactless payment here?
Come faccio a usare il pagamento senza contatto qui?
Koh-meh fah-choh ah oo-sah-reh eel pah-gah-men-toh sehn-zah kohn-taht-toh kwee?

Is there a limit to how much I can pay with my card?
C'è un limite a quanto posso pagare con la mia carta?
Cheh oon lee-mee-teh ah kwahn-toh pohs-soh pah-gah-reh kohn lah meeah kar-tah?

Do electronic payments require a PIN?
I pagamenti elettronici richiedono un PIN?
Ee pah-gah-men-tee eh-let-troh-nee-chee ree-kyeh-doh-noh oon PEEN?

Can I pay in installments here?
Posso pagare a rate qui?
Pohs-soh pah-gah-reh ah rah-teh kwee?

Are there any discounts for electronic payments?
Ci sono sconti per i pagamenti elettronici?
Chee soh-noh skohn-tee pehr ee pah-gah-men-tee eh-let-troh-nee-chee?

How can I check my card's balance?
Come posso controllare il saldo della mia carta?
*Koh-meh pohs-soh kohn-trohl-lah-reh eel sahl-doh dehl-lah
meeah kar-tah?*

What's the exchange rate for using my card abroad?
Qual è il tasso di cambio per usare la mia carta all'estero?
*Kwahl eh eel tahs-soh dee kahm-byoh pehr oo-sah-reh lah
meeah kar-tah ahl-leh-steh-roh?*

Can I withdraw money from my PayPal account here?
Posso prelevare denaro dal mio conto PayPal qui?
*Pohs-soh preh-leh-vah-reh deh-nah-roh dahl meeo kohn-toh
Pay-Pal kwee?*

Do you need my ID for card payments?
Avete bisogno della mia identità per i pagamenti con carta?
*Ah-veh-teh bee-zoh-nyoh dehl-lah meeah ee-den-tee-tah pehr
ee pah-gah-men-tee kohn kar-tah?*

How secure are online payments?
Quanto sono sicuri i pagamenti online?
*Kwahn-toh soh-noh see-koo-ree ee pah-gah-men-tee ohn-lee-
neh?*

Can I change my payment method after ordering?
Posso cambiare il metodo di pagamento dopo aver ordinato?
*Pohs-soh kahm-byah-reh eel meh-toh-doh dee pah-gah-men-
toh doh-poh ah-veh-reh ohr-dee-nah-toh?*

Elevator

Is the elevator working?
Dove si trova l'ascensore più vicino?
Do-veh see troh-vah lah-shen-soh-reh pyoo vee-chee-noh?

How do I call the elevator?
Come faccio a chiamare l'ascensore?
Koh-meh fah-choh ah kee-ah-mah-re lah-shen-soh-reh?

Is there an elevator in this building?
C'è un ascensore in questo edificio?
Tcheh oon ah-shen-soh-reh een kwes-toh eh-dee-fee-cho?

Can this elevator fit a wheelchair?
Questo ascensore può contenere una sedia a rotelle?
Kwes-toh ah-shen-soh-reh pwah kon-teh-neh-reh oo-nah se-dee-ah ah roh-tel-leh?

What is the maximum capacity of the elevator?
Qual è la capacità massima dell'ascensore?
Kwah-leh lah kah-pah-chee-tah mahs-see-mah del-lah-shen-soh-reh?

Does the elevator go to the rooftop?
L'ascensore arriva sul tetto?
Lah-shen-soh-reh ah-ree-vah sool teh-toh?

Is there a service elevator for luggage?
C'è un ascensore di servizio per i bagagli?
Tcheh oon ah-shen-soh-reh dee sehr-vee-tsyoh pehr ee bah-gahl-yee?

How many floors does the elevator serve?
Quanti piani serve l'ascensore?
Kwan-tee pee-ah-nee sehr-veh lah-shen-soh-reh?

Is the elevator to the left or right?
L'ascensore è a sinistra o a destra?
Lah-shen-soh-reh eh ah see-nee-strah oh ah deh-strah?

Are there stairs as an alternative to the elevator?
Ci sono scale come alternativa all'ascensore?
Tchee soh-noh skah-leh koh-meh ahl-tehr-nah-tee-vah ahl-lah-shen-soh-reh?

Is the elevator key-operated?
L'ascensore funziona con una chiave?
Lah-shen-soh-reh foon-tsyoh-nah kohn oo-nah kee-ah-veh?

Does the elevator have a stop button?
L'ascensore ha un pulsante di stop?
Lah-shen-soh-reh ah oon pool-sahn-teh dee stop?

Is the elevator accessible 24/7?
L'ascensore è accessibile 24 ore su 24?
Lah-shen-soh-reh eh ahk-tcheh-see-bee-leh ven-tee-kwa-troh oh-reh soo ven-tee-kwa-troh?

How long does it take for the elevator to arrive?
Quanto tempo ci vuole perché l'ascensore arrivi?
Kwan-toh tem-poh chee vwoh-leh pehr-keh lah-shen-soh-reh ah-ree-vee?

Can I use the elevator during a power outage?
Posso usare l'ascensore durante un'interruzione di corrente?
Pohs-soh oo-zah-reh lah-shen-soh-reh door-ahn-teh oon-een-teh-roop-tsyoh-neh dee koh-rren-teh?

Is there a charge for using the elevator?
C'è una tariffa per usare l'ascensore?
Tcheh oo-nah tah-ree-fah pehr oo-zah-reh lah-shen-soh-reh?

Are pets allowed in the elevator?
Gli animali sono ammessi nell'ascensore?
Glee ah-nee-mah-lee soh-noh ahm-mehs-see nel-lah-shen-soh-reh?

Does the elevator have a voice announcement system?
L'ascensore ha un sistema di annunci vocali?
Lah-shen-soh-reh ah oon see-steh-mah dee ahn-noon-tsee voh-kah-lee?

Where is the emergency phone in the elevator?
Dove si trova il telefono di emergenza nell'ascensore?
Do-veh see troh-vah eel teh-leh-foh-noh dee eh-mehr-jen-tsah nel-lah-shen-soh-reh?

Is it safe to use the elevator in case of fire?
È sicuro usare l'ascensore in caso di fuoco?
Eh see-koo-roh oo-zah-reh lah-shen-soh-reh een kah-zoh dee fwoh-koh?

Emergencies

Where is the nearest hospital?
Dove è l'ospedale più vicino?
Do-veh eh eel os-peh-dah-leh pyoo vee-chee-noh?

Can you call an ambulance?
Puoi chiamare un'ambulanza?
Pwoh-ee kee-ah-mah-reh oon ahm-boo-lahn-tsah?

I need a doctor.
Ho bisogno di un dottore.
Oh bee-soh-nyoh dee oon doh-toh-reh.

Is there a pharmacy nearby?
C'è una farmacia nelle vicinanze?
Cheh oo-nah far-mah-chee-ah neh-leh vee-chee-nahn-tseh?

I lost my passport.
Ho perso il mio passaporto.
Oh pehr-soh eel mee-oh pah-sah-por-toh.

I need help.
Ho bisogno di aiuto.
Oh bee-soh-nyoh dee ah-yoo-toh.

Is there a police station nearby?
C'è una stazione di polizia nelle vicinanze?
Cheh oo-nah stah-tsee-oh-neh dee poh-lee-tsee-ah neh-leh vee-chee-nahn-tseh?

Can you help me?
Puoi aiutarmi?
Pwoh-ee ah-yoo-tahr-mee?

I am lost.
Mi sono perso.
Mee soh-noh pehr-soh.

Where can I find a taxi?
Dove posso trovare un taxi?
Do-veh pohs-soh troh-vah-reh oon tahk-see?

How do I call the police?
Come faccio a chiamare la polizia?
Koh-meh fah-cho ah kee-ah-mah-reh lah poh-lee-tsee-ah?

I have a medical emergency.
Ho un'emergenza medica.
Oh oon-eh-mehr-jehn-tsah meh-dee-kah.

Can you show me the way to the nearest embassy?
Puoi mostrarmi la strada per l'ambasciata più vicina?
Pwoh-ee moh-strahr-mee lah strah-dah pehr l'ahm-bah-shah-tah pyoo vee-chee-nah?

I need an interpreter.
Ho bisogno di un interprete.
Oh bee-soh-nyoh dee oon een-tehr-preh-teh.

Can I use your phone?
Posso usare il tuo telefono?
Pohs-soh oo-zah-reh eel too-oh teh-leh-foh-noh?

Do you have a first aid kit?
Hai un kit di primo soccorso?
Ahy oon keet dee pree-moh soh-kohr-soh?

I am allergic to...
Sono allergico a...
Soh-noh ah-lehr-jee-koh ah...

Where is the nearest fire station?
Dove è la stazione dei vigili del fuoco più vicina?
Do-veh eh lah stah-tsee-oh-neh day vee-jee-lee dehl fwoh-koh pyoo vee-chee-nah?

I need to report a theft.
Devo denunciare un furto.
Deh-voh deh-noon-tsee-ah-reh oon foor-toh.

How can I get emergency medical assistance?
Come posso ottenere assistenza medica di emergenza?
Koh-meh pohs-soh oht-teh-neh-reh ah-see-stehn-tsah meh-dee-kah dee eh-mehr-jehn-tsah?

Fish

Salmon
Salmone
Sahl-moh-neh

Tuna
Tonno
Tohn-noh

Trout
Trota
Troh-tah

Cod
Merluzzo
Mer-loot-tsoh

Shrimp
Gamberetto
Gahm-beh-ret-toh

Lobster
Aragosta
Ah-rah-goh-stah

Crab
Granchio
Grahn-kyoh

Squid
Calamaro
Kah-lah-mah-roh

Octopus
Polpo
Pohl-poh

Clams
Vongole
Vohn-goh-leh

Mussels
Cozze
Kot-tseh

Sea Bass
Branzino
Brahn-tsee-noh

Swordfish
Pesce spada
Peh-sheh spah-dah

Anchovy
Acciuga
Ah-choo-gah

Herring
Aringa
Ah-reen-gah

Mackerel
Sgombro
Sgom-broh

Snapper
Dentice
Den-tee-cheh

Eel
Anguilla
An-gweel-lah

Scallop
Capesante
Kah-peh-sahn-teh

Flounder
Passera di mare
Pahs-seh-rah dee mah-reh

Fruit

Apple
Mela
Meh-lah

Banana
Banana
Bah-nah-nah

Orange
Arancia
Ah-rahn-cha

Strawberry
Fragola
Frah-go-lah

Grape
Uva
Oo-vah

Pineapple
Ananas
Ah-nah-nahs

Watermelon
Anguria
An-goo-ree-ah

Cherry
Ciliegia
Chee-lee-eh-jah

Pear
Pera

Peh-rah

Lemon
Limone
Lee-moh-neh

Peach
Pesca
Peh-skah

Mango
Mango
Mahn-go

Kiwi
Kiwi
Kee-wee

Grapefruit
Pompelmo
Pohm-pehl-moh

Blueberry
Mirtillo
Meer-tee-loh

Coconut
Cocco
Koh-koh

Apricot
Albicocca
Al-bee-koh-kah

Fig
Fico
Fee-koh

Pomegranate
Melograno
Meh-loh-grah-noh

Plum
Prugna
Proo-nyah

Gas Station

Where is the nearest gas station?
Dove è la stazione di servizio più vicina?
Do-veh eh lah stah-tsee-oh-neh dee sehr-vee-tsee-oh pyoo vee-chee-nah?

How do I get to the closest gas station?
Come arrivo alla stazione di servizio più vicina?
Co-meh ah-ree-voh ahl-lah stah-tsee-oh-neh dee sehr-vee-tsee-oh pyoo vee-chee-nah?

Is there a gas station open 24 hours nearby?
C'è una stazione di servizio aperta 24 ore nelle vicinanze?
Tcheh oo-nah stah-tsee-oh-neh dee sehr-vee-tsee-oh ah-pehr-tah ven-tee-kwaht-troh oh-reh nel-leh vee-chee-nahn-tseh?

Can I pay with a credit card at this gas station?
Posso pagare con carta di credito in questa stazione di servizio?
Pohs-soh pah-gah-reh kohn kahr-tah dee kreh-dee-toh een kweh-stah stah-tsee-oh-neh dee sehr-vee-tsee-oh?

Do you have unleaded gasoline?
Avete benzina senza piombo?
Ah-veh-teh behn-tsee-nah sehn-zah pee-ohm-boh?

What is the price of diesel here?
Qual è il prezzo del diesel qui?
Kwah-l eh eel preht-tsoh dehl dee-eh-zehl kwee?

Is self-service available at this station?
È disponibile il self-service in questa stazione?
Eh dees-poh-nee-bee-leh eel self-ser-vee-tcheh een kweh-stah stah-tsee-oh-neh?

Where can I find an air pump?
Dove posso trovare una pompa d'aria?
Do-veh pohs-soh troh-vah-reh oo-nah pohm-pah dah-ree-ah?

Do you sell motor oil?
Vendete olio motore?
Ven-deh-teh oh-lee-oh moh-toh-reh?

Can I use the restroom here?
Posso usare il bagno qui?
Pohs-soh oo-sah-reh eel bah-nyoh kwee?

How much does it cost to fill up the tank?
Quanto costa fare il pieno?
Kwahn-toh koh-stah fah-reh eel pyeh-noh?

Do you offer car wash services?
Offrite servizi di lavaggio auto?
Ohf-free-teh sehr-vee-tsee dee lah-vah-joh ow-toh?

Is it possible to check the tire pressure?
È possibile controllare la pressione delle gomme?
Eh pohs-see-bee-leh kohn-trohl-lah-reh lah prehs-see-oh-neh dehl-leh gohm-meh?

Where can I buy a road map?
Dove posso comprare una mappa stradale?
Do-veh pohs-soh kom-prah-reh oo-nah mahp-pah strah-dah-leh?

Do you have a loyalty program?
Avete un programma fedeltà?
Ah-veh-teh oon proh-grahm-mah feh-del-tah?

Can I get a receipt, please?
Posso avere uno scontrino, per favore?

Pohs-soh ah-veh-reh oo-noh skohn-tree-noh, pehr fah-voh-reh?

Is there an electric vehicle charging station?
C'è una stazione di ricarica per veicoli elettrici?
Tcheh oo-nah stah-tsee-oh-neh dee ree-kah-ree-kah pehr veh-ee-koh-lee eh-leh-tree-chee?

How do I operate the pump?
Come si usa la pompa?
Co-meh see oo-sah lah pohm-pah?

Can I buy snacks here?
Posso comprare degli snack qui?
Pohs-soh kom-prah-reh dehl-ee snahk kwee?

Where should I park while refueling?
Dove dovrei parcheggiare mentre faccio rifornimento?
Do-veh doh-vreh-ee pahrk-geh-yah-reh men-treh fah-tchoh ree-fohr-nee-men-toh?

Get to Know Someone (General)

What's your name?
Come ti chiami?
Koh-meh tee kyah-mee?

Where are you from?
Di dove sei?
Dee doh-veh say?

How old are you?
Quanti anni hai?
Kwan-tee ahn-nee ahy?

Do you live here?
Vivi qui?
Vee-vee kwee?

What do you do for a living?
Che lavoro fai?
Keh lah-voh-roh fahy?

Do you like it here?
Ti piace qui?
Tee pyah-cheh kwee?

What's your hobby?
Qual è il tuo hobby?
Kwah-l eh eel twoh ohb-bee?

What kind of music do you like?
Che tipo di musica ti piace?
Keh tee-poh dee moo-zee-kah tee pyah-cheh?

Have you been here long?
Sei qui da molto?
Say kwee dah mol-toh?

What's your favorite food?
Qual è il tuo cibo preferito?
Kwah-l eh eel twoh chee-boh preh-feh-ree-toh?

Do you have any siblings?
Hai fratelli o sorelle?
Ahy frah-tel-lee oh soh-rel-leh?

What are you passionate about?
Cosa ti appassiona?
Koh-sah tee ah-pahs-syo-nah?

Can you recommend a good restaurant?
Puoi consigliare un buon ristorante?
Pwoh-ee kon-see-lyah-reh oon bwon ree-stoh-rahn-teh?

What movies do you like?
Che film ti piacciono?
Keh feelm tee pyahc-choh-noh?

What brings you here?
Cosa ti porta qui?
Koh-sah tee pohr-tah kwee?

Have you traveled to other countries?
Hai viaggiato in altri paesi?
Ahy vee-ah-jah-toh een ahl-tree pah-eh-zee?

What's your favorite book?
Qual è il tuo libro preferito?
Kwah-l eh eel twoh lee-broh preh-feh-ree-toh?

Do you play any sports?
Pratichi qualche sport?
Prah-tee-kee kwahl-keh spohrt?

What's your favorite way to spend time?
Come preferisci trascorrere il tempo?
Koh-meh preh-feh-ree-shee trahs-kohr-reh eel tem-poh?

Can you tell me more about your culture?
Puoi dirmi di più sulla tua cultura?
Pwoh-ee deer-mee dee pyoo soo-lah twoah kool-too-rah?

Getting to Know Someone New and Introducing Yourself

What's your name?
Come ti chiami?
Co-meh tee kee-ah-mee?

How old are you?
Quanti anni hai?
Kwan-tee an-nee ai?

Where are you from?
Di dove sei?
Dee do-veh say?

Do you speak English?
Parli inglese?
Par-lee een-gleh-seh?

I am here on vacation.
Sono qui in vacanza.
So-noh kwee een va-cahn-tsah.

I am traveling with my family.
Sto viaggiando con la mia famiglia.
Stoh vee-ah-jan-doh kon lah mee-ah fa-meel-yah.

I am here for work.
Sono qui per lavoro.
So-noh kwee pehr lah-vo-roh.

Can I have your phone number?
Posso avere il tuo numero di telefono?
Pohs-soh ah-veh-reh eel two-oh noo-meh-roh dee teh-leh-foh-noh?

Do you have Instagram?
Hai Instagram?
Eye een-stah-gram?

What do you do for a living?
Cosa fai di mestiere?
Koh-sah fai dee meh-stee-eh-reh?

I love traveling.
Mi piace viaggiare.
Mee pee-ah-cheh vee-ah-jah-reh.

My favorite hobby is reading.
Il mio hobby preferito è leggere.
Eel mee-oh ob-bee preh-feh-ree-toh eh leh-jeh-reh.

I am allergic to peanuts.
Sono allergico alle arachidi.
So-noh al-ler-jee-koh al-leh ah-rah-kee-dee.

I am a vegetarian.
Sono vegetariano.
So-noh veh-jeh-tah-ree-ah-noh.

I am studying Italian.
Sto studiando l'italiano.
Stoh stoo-dee-ahn-doh lee-tah-lee-ah-noh.

I like Italian cuisine.
Mi piace la cucina italiana.
Mee pee-ah-cheh lah koo-chee-nah ee-tah-lee-ah-nah.

I am here to learn Italian.
Sono qui per imparare l'italiano.
So-noh kwee pehr eem-pah-rah-reh lee-tah-lee-ah-noh.

Can you recommend a good restaurant?
Puoi consigliare un buon ristorante?
Pwoh-ee kon-seel-yah-reh oon bwon ree-stoh-rahn-teh?

I would like to make some friends here.
Vorrei fare amicizia qui.
Vohr-ray fah-reh ah-mee-chee-tsya kwee.

Can you take a picture of me, please?
Puoi farmi una foto, per favore?
Pwoh-ee far-mee oo-nah foh-toh, pehr fah-vo-reh?

Hotel

Do you have a room available?
Avete una camera disponibile?
Ah-veh-teh oo-nah kah-meh-rah dee-spoh-nee-bee-leh?

Can I check in now?
Posso fare il check-in ora?
Pohs-soh fah-reh eel chehk-een oh-rah?

What time is breakfast?
A che ora è la colazione?
Ah keh oh-rah eh lah koh-lah-tsyoh-neh?

Can I have the Wi-Fi password?
Posso avere la password del Wi-Fi?
Pohs-soh ah-veh-reh lah pahs-swuhrd dehl Wee-Fee?

Where is the gym?
Dove si trova la palestra?
Doh-veh see troh-vah lah pah-leh-strah?

Is there a pool?
C'è una piscina?
Cheh oo-nah pees-chee-nah?

Can you wake me up at 7 AM?
Potete svegliarmi alle 7 del mattino?
Poh-teh-teh svehl-yahr-mee ahl-leh seht-teh dehl maht-tee-noh?

How do I get to the city center?
Come faccio ad arrivare al centro città?
Koh-meh fah-tchoh ah ah-rree-vah-reh ahl chen-troh chee-tah?

Can I have an extra pillow?
Posso avere un cuscino in più?
Pohs-soh ah-veh-reh oon koos-chee-noh een pyoo?

What's the checkout time?
Qual è l'orario del checkout?
Kwah-leh loh-rah-ree-oh dehl chehk-owt?

Is breakfast included?
La colazione è inclusa?
Lah koh-lah-tsyoh-neh eh een-kloo-sah?

Can you call me a taxi?
Potete chiamarmi un taxi?
Poh-teh-teh kee-ah-mahr-mee oon tahk-see?

Do you have a map of the city?
Avete una mappa della città?
Ah-veh-teh oo-nah mahp-pah dehl-lah chee-tah?

Can I leave my luggage here?
Posso lasciare qui i miei bagagli?
Pohs-soh lah-shee-ah-reh kwee ee mee-eh-ee bah-gahl-yee?

Do you offer laundry service?
Offrite il servizio di lavanderia?
Ohf-free-teh eel sehr-vee-tsyoh dee lah-vahn-deh-ree-ah?

How much does a room cost per night?
Quanto costa una camera per notte?
Kwahn-toh koh-stah oo-nah kah-meh-rah pehr noht-teh?

Can I have the room cleaned?
Posso fare pulire la camera?
Pohs-soh fah-reh poo-lee-reh lah kah-meh-rah?

Is there a restaurant in the hotel?
C'è un ristorante nell'hotel?
Cheh oon ree-stoh-rahn-teh nehl-loh-tehl?

Can I get an iron?
Posso avere un ferro da stiro?
Pohs-soh ah-veh-reh oon fehr-roh dah stee-roh?

Do you have a safe in the room?
C'è una cassaforte in camera?
Cheh oo-nah kahs-sah-fohr-teh een kah-meh-rah?

I Lost My Son/Daughter

I have lost my son. Can you help me?
Ho perso mio figlio. Puoi aiutarmi?
Oh pehr-soh mee-oh feel-yoh. Pwoh-ee ah-yoo-tar-mee?

I can't find my daughter. What should I do?
Non riesco a trovare mia figlia. Cosa dovrei fare?
Non ryeh-skoh ah troh-vah-reh mee-ah feel-yah. Koh-sah doh-vreh-ee fah-reh?

My child is missing. Who should I contact?
Mio figlio è scomparso. Chi dovrei contattare?
Mee-oh feel-yoh eh skom-pahr-soh. Kee doh-vreh-ee kon-tah-tah-reh?

Can you call the police for me? My son is lost.
Puoi chiamare la polizia per me? Mio figlio è perso.
Pwoh-ee kyah-mah-reh lah poh-lee-tzee-ah pehr meh? Mee-oh feel-yoh eh pehr-soh?

How do I report a lost child here?
Come faccio a segnalare un bambino perso qui?
Koh-meh fah-choh ah seh-nyah-lah-reh oon bam-bee-noh pehr-soh kwee?

My daughter didn't come back to our meeting point.
My daughter didn't come back to our meeting point.
Mia figlia non è tornata al nostro punto di incontro.
Mee-ah feel-yah non eh tor-nah-tah ahl noh-stroh poon-toh dee een-kohn-troh.

Could you help me look for my son?
Potresti aiutarmi a cercare mio figlio?
Poh-trehs-tee ah-yoo-tar-mee ah cher-kah-reh mee-oh feel-yoh?

I need to find my child quickly.
Devo trovare mio figlio rapidamente.
Deh-voh troh-vah-reh mee-oh feel-yoh rah-pee-dah-men-teh.

Who can I talk to about a missing child?
Con chi posso parlare di un bambino scomparso?
Kon kee pohs-soh pahr-lah-reh dee oon bam-bee-noh skom-pahr-soh?

My son was here a moment ago.
Mio figlio era qui un attimo fa.
Mee-oh feel-yoh eh-rah kwee oon ah-tee-moh fah.

I'm looking for my daughter.
Sto cercando mia figlia.
Stoh cher-kahn-doh mee-ah feel-yah.

Please, can someone help me find my child?
Per favore, può qualcuno aiutarmi a trovare mio figlio?
Pehr fah-voh-reh, pwoh kwahl-koo-noh ah-yoo-tar-mee ah troh-vah-reh mee-oh feel-yoh?

I need assistance. My daughter is not with me.
Ho bisogno di assistenza. Mia figlia non è con me.
Oh bee-zoh-nyoh dee ah-sees-ten-tsah. Mee-ah feel-yah non eh kon meh.

What's the procedure for a lost child in this area?
Qual è la procedura per un bambino perso in questa zona?
Kwahl eh lah proh-cheh-doo-rah pehr oon bam-bee-noh pehr-soh een kwehs-tah tsoh-nah?

Can we make an announcement about my missing son?
Possiamo fare un annuncio riguardo mio figlio scomparso?
Pohs-see-ah-moh fah-reh oon ahn-noon-tsee-oh ree-gwahr-doh mee-oh feel-yoh skom-pahr-soh?

Is there a lost and found here for children?
C'è un ufficio oggetti smarriti qui per bambini?
Ch'eh oon oo-fee-tchee ohj-jeh-tee smahr-ree-tee kwee pehr bam-bee-nee?

How can I describe my son to the authorities?
Come posso descrivere mio figlio alle autorità?
Koh-meh pohs-soh deh-skree-veh-reh mee-oh feel-yoh ah-lleh ah-oo-toh-ree-tah?

Please help me, my son has gone missing.
Per favore, aiutami, mio figlio è scomparso.
Pehr fah-voh-reh, ah-yoo-tah-mee, mee-oh feel-yoh eh skom-pahr-soh.

My daughter was supposed to meet me here.
Mia figlia doveva incontrarmi qui.
Mee-ah feel-yah doh-veh-vah een-kohn-trahr-mee kwee.

Who do I speak to if my child doesn't return?
A chi parlo se mio figlio non torna?
Ah kee pahr-loh seh mee-oh feel-yoh non tor-nah?

Laundry

Where is the nearest laundry?
Dove è la lavanderia più vicina?
Do-veh eh lah lah-vahn-deh-ree-ah pyoo vee-chee-nah?

How much does it cost to wash clothes?
Quanto costa lavare i vestiti?
Kwahn-toh koh-stah lah-vah-reh ee veh-stee-tee?

Do you offer dry cleaning services?
Offrite servizi di lavaggio a secco?
Ohf-free-teh sehr-vee-tsee dee lah-vahj-joh ah sehk-koh?

Can I get my clothes washed today?
Posso fare lavare i miei vestiti oggi?
Pohs-soh fah-reh lah-vah-reh ee mee-ey veh-stee-tee ohj-jee?

What time will my laundry be ready?
A che ora sarà pronta la mia biancheria?
Ah keh oh-rah sah-rah prohn-tah lah mee-ah bee-ahn-keh-ree-ah?

Is there a self-service laundry nearby?
C'è una lavanderia self-service nelle vicinanze?
Cheh oo-nah lah-vahn-deh-ree-ah self-sehr-vee-che neh-leh vee-chee-nahn-tseh?

How long does a washing cycle take?
Quanto tempo impiega un ciclo di lavaggio?
Kwahn-toh tem-poh eem-pyeh-gah oon chee-kloh dee lah-vahj-joh?

Do you use eco-friendly detergents?
Usate detergenti ecologici?
Oo-sah-teh deh-tehr-jehn-tee eh-koh-loh-jee-chee?

Can I pick up my laundry after hours?
Posso ritirare la mia biancheria dopo l'orario?
*Pohs-soh ree-tee-rah-reh lah mee-ah bee-ahn-keh-ree-ah
doh-poh loh-rah-ree-oh?*

Do you have a price list for laundry services?
Avete un listino prezzi per i servizi di lavanderia?
*Ah-veh-teh oon lees-tee-noh preht-tsee pehr ee sehr-vee-tsee
dee lah-vahn-deh-ree-ah?*

Is fabric softener used in washing?
Si usa l'ammorbidente nel lavaggio?
See oo-sah lam-mohr-bee-dehn-teh nel lah-vahj-joh?

How should I prepare my clothes for laundry?
Come devo preparare i miei vestiti per la lavanderia?
*Koh-meh deh-voh preh-pah-rah-reh ee mee-ey veh-stee-tee
pehr lah lah-vahn-deh-ree-ah?*

Are there any clothes that cannot be washed here?
Ci sono vestiti che non possono essere lavati qui?
*Chee soh-noh veh-stee-tee keh non pohs-soh-noh ehs-seh-reh
lah-vah-tee kwee?*

What are your operating hours?
Quali sono i vostri orari di apertura?
*Kwah-lee soh-noh ee voh-stree oh-rah-ree dee ah-pehr-too-
rah?*

Can I have a receipt for my laundry?
Posso avere una ricevuta per la mia lavanderia?
Pohs-soh ah-veh-reh oo-nah ree-cheh-voo-tah pehr lah mee-ah lah-vahn-deh-ree-ah?

Do you offer express laundry services?
Offrite servizi di lavanderia express?
Ohf-free-teh sehr-vee-tsee dee lah-vahn-deh-ree-ah ehks-prehss?

How do I pay for the laundry service?
Come pago il servizio di lavanderia?
Koh-meh pah-goh eel sehr-vee-tsee-oh dee lah-vahn-deh-ree-ah?

Is it possible to track my laundry order online?
È possibile tracciare il mio ordine di lavanderia online?
Eh pohs-see-bee-leh trah-chah-reh eel mee-oh ohr-dee-neh dee lah-vahn-deh-ree-ah ohn-lee-neh?

Do you separate whites and colors?
Separate i bianchi dai colorati?
Seh-pah-rah-teh ee byahn-kee dah-ee koh-loh-rah-tee?

What should I do if I'm not satisfied with the laundry service?
Cosa dovrei fare se non sono soddisfatto del servizio di lavanderia?
Koh-sah doh-vreh-ee fah-reh seh non soh-noh soh-dees-fah-toh del sehr-vee-tsee-oh dee lah-vahn-deh-ree-ah?

Luggage

Where can I store my luggage?
Dove posso depositare i miei bagagli?
Doh-veh pohs-soh deh-poh-see-tah-reh ee mee-eh ee bah-gahl-yee?

How much does it cost to check this bag?
Quanto costa imbarcare questa valigia?
Kwahn-toh koh-stah eem-bahr-kah-reh kweh-stah vah-lee-jah?

Is there a weight limit for luggage?
C'è un limite di peso per i bagagli?
Cheh oon lee-mee-teh dee peh-soh pehr ee bah-gahl-yee?

Can I carry this on the plane?
Posso portare questo a bordo dell'aereo?
Pohs-soh pohr-tah-reh kweh-stoh ah bohr-doh del-lah-eh-reh-oh?

Do you have luggage carts available?
Avete carrelli per bagagli disponibili?
Ah-veh-teh kahr-rel-lee pehr bah-gahl-yee dee-spoh-nee-bee-lee?

Can I lock my luggage?
Posso chiudere a chiave i miei bagagli?
Pohs-soh kyoo-deh-reh ah kyah-veh ee mee-eh ee bah-gahl-yee?

How do I claim my luggage?
Come faccio a ritirare i miei bagagli?
Koh-meh fah-tcho ah ree-tee-rah-reh ee mee-eh ee bah-gahl-yee?

Is my luggage insured?
I miei bagagli sono assicurati?
Ee mee-eh ee bah-gahl-yee soh-noh ah-see-coo-rah-tee?

Where is the luggage claim area?
Dove si trova l'area di ritiro bagagli?
Doh-veh see troh-vah lah-reh-ah dee ree-tee-roh bah-gahl-yee?

Can I get help with my luggage?
Posso avere aiuto con i miei bagagli?
Pohs-soh ah-veh-reh ah-yoo-toh kohn ee mee-eh ee bah-gahl-yee?

What's the policy on oversized luggage?
Qual è la politica per il bagaglio sovradimensionato?
Kwah-leh lah poh-lee-tee-kah pehr eel bah-gahl-yoh soh-vrah-dee-mehn-syah-toh?

Did my luggage make it on the flight?
I miei bagagli sono stati imbarcati sul volo?
Ee mee-eh ee bah-gahl-yee soh-noh stah-tee eem-bahr-kah-tee sool voh-loh?

Why was my luggage delayed?
Perché i miei bagagli sono stati ritardati?
Pehr-keh ee mee-eh ee bah-gahl-yee soh-noh stah-tee ree-tahr-dah-tee?

Can I bring this as carry-on luggage?
Posso portare questo come bagaglio a mano?
Pohs-soh pohr-tah-reh kweh-stoh koh-meh bah-gahl-yoh ah mah-noh?

How do I report lost luggage?
Come faccio a segnalare i bagagli persi?
Koh-meh fah-tcho ah seh-nyah-lah-reh ee bah-gahl-yee pehr-see?

Where do I drop off my luggage for the flight?
Dove devo lasciare i miei bagagli per il volo?
Doh-veh deh-voh lah-shee-ah-reh ee mee-eh ee bah-gahl-yee pehr eel voh-loh?

Can I track my luggage?
Posso tracciare i miei bagagli?
Pohs-soh trah-chah-reh ee mee-eh ee bah-gahl-yee?

What do I do if my luggage is damaged?
Cosa faccio se i miei bagagli sono danneggiati?
Koh-sah fah-tcho seh ee mee-eh ee bah-gahl-yee soh-noh dahn-neh-jah-tee?

Is there a service to wrap my luggage?
C'è un servizio per incellofanare i miei bagagli?
Cheh oon sehr-vee-tsyoh pehr een-tcheh-loh-fah-nah-reh ee mee-eh ee bah-gahl-yee?

Are there any restrictions on what I can pack?
Ci sono restrizioni su ciò che posso imballare?
Chee soh-noh reh-stree-tsyoh-nee soo choh keh pohs-soh eem-bahl-lah-reh?

Making a Phone Call

Phone Number
Numero di telefono
Noo-meh-roh dee teh-leh-foh-noh

Can I use your phone?
Posso usare il tuo telefono?
Pohs-soh oo-zah-reh eel twoh teh-leh-foh-noh?

I need to make a call.
Devo fare una chiamata.
Deh-voh fah-reh oo-nah kyah-mah-tah

How do I dial an international number?
Come faccio a comporre un numero internazionale?
Koh-meh fah-choh ah kom-pohr-reh oon noo-meh-roh een-ter-nah-tsyoh-nah-leh?

Is there a phone booth nearby?
C'è una cabina telefonica qui vicino?
Cheh oo-nah kah-bee-nah teh-leh-foh-nee-kah kwee vee-chee-noh?

I need a phone card.
Ho bisogno di una scheda telefonica.
Oh bee-zoh-nyoh dee oo-nah skeh-dah teh-leh-foh-nee-kah

My phone battery is dead.
La batteria del mio telefono è scarica.
Lah bat-teh-ree-ah del mee-oh teh-leh-foh-noh eh skah-ree-kah

Do you have a charger?
Hai un caricabatterie?
Ahy oon kah-ree-kah-bat-teh-ree-eh?

I need to send a text message.
Devo inviare un messaggio.
Deh-voh een-vyah-reh oon mes-sahj-joh

How much does it cost to call...?
Quanto costa chiamare...?
Kwahn-toh koh-stah kyah-mah-reh...?

Do you have coverage here?
Hai campo qui?
Ahy kahm-poh kwee?

The call dropped.
La chiamata è caduta.
Lah kyah-mah-tah eh kah-doo-tah

I can't hear you well.
Non ti sento bene.
Nohn tee seen-toh beh-neh

My number is...
Il mio numero è...
Eel mee-oh noo-meh-roh eh...

Please call me back.
Per favore richiamami.
Pehr fah-voh-reh ree-kyah-mah-mee

I'm trying to reach...
Sto cercando di contattare...
Stoh cher-kahn-doh dee kon-tah-tah-reh...

The line is busy.
La linea è occupata.
Lah lee-neh-ah eh ok-koo-pah-tah

Can I leave a message?
Posso lasciare un messaggio?
Pohs-soh lah-syah-reh oon mes-sahj-joh?

How do I check my voicemail?
Come faccio a controllare la mia segreteria?
Koh-meh fah-choh ah kon-trohl-lah-reh lah mee-ah seh-greh-teh-ree-ah?

I need to recharge my phone.
Devo ricaricare il mio telefono.
Deh-voh ree-kah-ree-kah-reh eel mee-oh teh-leh-foh-noh

Making Yourself Understood

Do you speak English?
Parli inglese?
Par-lee een-gleh-seh?

Where is the bathroom?
Dove è il bagno?
Doh-veh eh eel bah-nyoh?

I need help.
Ho bisogno di aiuto.
Oh bee-zoh-nyoh dee ah-yoo-toh.

I'm lost.
Mi sono perso.
Mee soh-noh pehr-soh.

Can I pay with a credit card?
Posso pagare con una carta di credito?
Pohs-soh pah-gah-reh kohn oo-nah kar-tah dee kreh-dee-toh?

How much is this?
Quanto costa questo?
Kwahn-toh koh-stah kweh-stoh?

I would like a coffee.
Vorrei un caffè.
Vohr-ray oon kahf-feh.

Can I have the menu, please?
Posso avere il menù, per favore?
Pohs-soh ah-veh-reh eel meh-noo, pehr fah-voh-reh?

Where can I buy a ticket?
Dove posso comprare un biglietto?
Doh-veh pohs-soh kohm-prah-reh oon bee-lyet-toh?

Is there a pharmacy nearby?
C'è una farmacia qui vicino?
Cheh oo-nah far-mah-chee-ah kwee vee-chee-noh?

Can you recommend a restaurant?
Puoi consigliarmi un ristorante?
Pwoh-ee kohn-sil-yar-mee oon ree-stoh-rahn-teh?

I'm allergic to peanuts.
Sono allergico alle arachidi.
Soh-noh al-ler-jee-koh ahl-leh ah-rah-kee-dee.

Please call an ambulance.
Per favore, chiama un'ambulanza.
Pehr fah-voh-reh, kee-ah-mah oon-am-boo-lahn-tsah.

Can you help me find a hotel?
Puoi aiutarmi a trovare un albergo?
Pwoh-ee ah-yoo-tar-mee ah troh-vah-reh oon al-ber-goh?

I'd like to exchange money.
Vorrei cambiare dei soldi.
Vohr-ray kahm-bee-ah-reh day sohl-dee.

Can I get a map?
Posso avere una mappa?
Pohs-soh ah-veh-reh oo-nah mahp-pah?

Where is the nearest ATM?
Dove è il bancomat più vicino?
Doh-veh eh eel bahn-koh-maht pyoo vee-chee-noh?

How do I get to the airport?

Come faccio ad arrivare all'aeroporto?

Koh-meh fah-choh ah ah-rree-vah-reh ahl-lah-eh-roh-por-toh?

Is this the right way to the train station?

È questa la strada giusta per la stazione ferroviaria?

Eh kweh-stah lah strah-dah joo-stah pehr lah stah-tsyoh-neh fehr-roh-vee-ah-ree-ah?

Malfunctions and Repairs

It's not working.
Non funziona.
Non foon-tsyoh-nah

It's broken.
È rotto.
Eh roht-toh

Can it be fixed?
È riparabile?
Eh ree-pah-rah-bee-leh?

Where can I find a repair shop?
Dove posso trovare una officina?
Doh-veh pohs-so troh-vah-reh oo-nah oh-fee-chee-nah?

I need a mechanic.
Ho bisogno di un meccanico.
Oh bee-zoh-nyoh dee oon mek-kah-nee-koh

Can you help me jumpstart the car?
Puoi aiutarmi a fare partire la macchina con i cavi?
Pwoh-ee ah-yoo-tahr-mee ah fah-reh pahr-tee-reh lah mack-kee-nah kon ee kah-vee?

I have a flat tire.
Ho una gomma a terra.
Oh oo-nah gom-mah ah teh-rrah

Do you have a spare part?
Avete un pezzo di ricambio?
Ah-veh-teh oon peht-tso dee ree-kahm-byoh?

The air conditioning is not cooling.
L'aria condizionata non raffredda.
Lah-ree-ah kon-dee-tsyoh-nah-tah non rahf-freh-dah

Where can I recharge the battery?
Dove posso ricaricare la batteria?
Doh-veh pohs-so ree-kah-ree-kah-reh lah bat-teh-ree-ah?

The screen is cracked.
Lo schermo è rotto.
Loh sker-moh eh roht-toh

Is there a warranty?
C'è una garanzia?
Cheh oo-nah gah-rahn-tsee-ah?

How long will the repair take?
Quanto tempo ci vorrà per la riparazione?
Kwahn-toh tem-poh chee vohr-rah pehr lah ree-pah-rah-tsyoh-neh?

I lost my charger.
Ho perso il mio caricatore.
Oh pehr-soh eel mee-oh kah-ree-kah-toh-reh

The water is not heating up.
L'acqua non si scalda.
Lahk-kwah non see skal-dah

Do you have tools I could use?
Avete attrezzi che posso usare?
Ah-veh-teh at-tret-tsee keh pohs-so oo-zah-reh?

The Wi-Fi is not connecting.
Il Wi-Fi non si collega.
Eel wee-fee non see kohl-leh-gah

I need to reset my password.
Devo reimpostare la mia password.
Deh-voh ray-eem-poh-stah-reh lah mee-ah pass-word

There's a leak.
C'è una perdita.
Cheh oo-nah pehr-dee-tah

The light is not turning on.
La luce non si accende.
Lah loo-cheh non see ahc-chen-deh

Men's Clothing Shopping

Do you have this in a larger size?
Avete questo in una taglia più grande?
Ah-veh-teh kwes-toh een oo-nah tah-lyah pyoo grahn-deh?

Can I try this on?
Posso provarlo?
Pohs-soh proh-vahr-loh?

Where can I find men's shoes?
Dove posso trovare scarpe da uomo?
Do-veh pohs-soh troh-vahr-reh skar-peh dah oooh-moh?

I'm looking for a suit.
Cerco un abito.
Chair-koh oon ah-bee-toh.

Do you sell ties?
Vendete cravatte?
Ven-deh-teh kra-vat-teh?

I need a belt.
Ho bisogno di una cintura.
Oh bee-zoh-nyoh dee oo-nah cheen-too-rah.

Is this waterproof?
È impermeabile?
Eh eem-per-meh-ah-bee-leh?

Do you have a fitting room?
Avete un camerino?
Ah-veh-teh oon kah-meh-ree-noh?

How much does this jacket cost?
Quanto costa questa giacca?
Kwahn-toh koh-stah kwes-tah jahk-kah?

Can I get a discount?
Posso avere uno sconto?
Pohs-soh ah-veh-reh oo-noh skon-toh?

I'm looking for a leather jacket.
Cerco una giacca di pelle.
Chair-koh oo-nah jahk-kah dee pehl-leh.

Are these pants available in (color)
Questi pantaloni sono disponibili in (colore)?
Kwes-tee pahn-tah-loh-nee soh-noh dee-spoh-nee-bee-lee een neh-roh?

I would like to buy a watch.
Vorrei comprare un orologio.
Vohr-ray kom-prah-reh oon oh-roh-loh-joh.

Where are the casual shirts?
Dove sono le camicie casual?
Do-veh soh-noh leh kah-mee-cheh kah-zwahl?

Do you have silk scarves?
Avete sciarpe di seta?
Ah-veh-teh shahr-peh dee seh-tah?

I need a pair of sunglasses.
Ho bisogno di un paio di occhiali da sole.
Oh bee-zoh-nyoh dee oon pah-yoh dee ok-kee-ah-lee dah soh-leh.

Are these socks made of cotton?
Questi calzini sono di cotone?
Kwes-tee kal-tsee-nee soh-noh dee koh-toh-neh?

I'm looking for a winter coat.
Cerco un cappotto invernale.
Chair-koh oon kahp-pot-toh een-vehr-nah-leh.

Where can I find a hat?
Dove posso trovare un cappello?
Do-veh pohs-soh troh-vahr-reh oon kahp-pehl-loh?

Do you have wool sweaters?
Avete maglioni di lana?
Ah-veh-teh mah-lyoh-nee dee lah-nah?

Mountain

Where is the nearest mountain?
Dove è la montagna più vicina?
Do-veh eh lah mon-tah-nyah pyoo vee-chee-nah?

How do I get to the mountain?
Come faccio ad arrivare alla montagna?
Ko-meh fah-cho ad ah-rree-vah-reh ah-lah mon-tah-nyah?

What is the height of this mountain?
Qual è l'altezza di questa montagna?
Kwah-l eh lahl-teh-tsah dee kweh-stah mon-tah-nyah?

Is it safe to hike here?
È sicuro fare escursioni qui?
Eh see-koo-roh fah-reh eh-skoo-rsee-oh-nee kwee?

Do I need special equipment for the hike?
Ho bisogno di attrezzature speciali per l'escursione?
Oh bee-zoh-nyoh dee at-treht-tsah-too-reh speh-chah-lee pehr leh-skoo-rsee-oh-neh?

What's the best time to climb the mountain?
Qual è il miglior momento per scalare la montagna?
Kwah-l eh eel meel-yohr moh-men-toh pehr skah-lah-reh lah mon-tah-nyah?

Are there guided tours available?
Ci sono tour guidati disponibili?
Chee soh-noh toor gwee-dah-tee dee-spo-nee-bee-lee?

How long does the hike take?
Quanto tempo ci vuole per fare l'escursione?
Kwahn-toh tem-poh chee vwoh-leh pehr fah-reh leh-skoo-rsee-oh-neh?

Is there a map of the hiking trails?
C'è una mappa dei sentieri per escursioni?
Cheh oo-nah mahp-pah dey sen-tee-ree pehr eh-skoo-rsee-oh-nee?

Can I camp in the mountains?
Posso accamparmi in montagna?
Pohs-soh ah-kahm-par-mee een mon-tah-nyah?

What wildlife can I see in the mountains?
Quali animali selvatici posso vedere in montagna?
Kwah-lee ah-nee-mah-lee sel-vah-tee-chee pohs-soh veh-deh-reh een mon-tah-nyah?

Are there any mountain restaurants?
Ci sono ristoranti in montagna?
Chee soh-noh ree-stoh-rahn-tee een mon-tah-nyah?

Do I need a permit to hike here?
Ho bisogno di un permesso per fare escursioni qui?
Oh bee-zoh-nyoh dee oon pehr-mehs-soh pehr fah-reh eh-skoo-rsee-oh-nee kwee?

What is the difficulty level of the trails?
Qual è il livello di difficoltà dei sentieri?
Kwah-l eh eel lee-vehl-loh dee dee-fee-kool-tah dey sen-tee-ree?

Can I rent equipment here?
Posso noleggiare attrezzature qui?
Pohs-soh noh-leh-jah-reh at-treht-tsah-too-reh kwee?

115

Where can I buy hiking gear?
Dove posso comprare attrezzatura per escursionismo?
*Do-veh pohs-soh kom-prah-reh at-treht-tsah-too-rah pehr
eh-skoo-see-oh-nee-smoh?*

Is there a rescue service in case of emergency?
C'è un servizio di soccorso in caso di emergenza?
*Cheh oon sehr-vee-tsee-oh dee soh-kohr-soh een kah-zoh dee
eh-mehr-jehn-tsah?*

How is the weather in the mountains?
Com'è il tempo in montagna?
Koh-meh eel tem-poh een mon-tah-nyah?

Are there any mountain lodges?
Ci sono rifugi in montagna?
Chee soh-noh ree-foo-jee een mon-tah-nyah?

Can I drink the water from the streams?
Posso bere l'acqua dei ruscelli?
Pohs-soh beh-reh lahk-wah dey roo-scheh-lee?

Museums

What are the museum's opening hours?
Dove sono gli orari di apertura del museo?
Do-veh soh-noh ly or-ah-ree dee ah-per-too-rah del moo-zeh-oh?

Is there a discount for students?
C'è uno sconto per gli studenti?
Cheh oo-noh skon-toh pehr ly stoo-den-tee?

Can I take pictures in the museum?
Posso fare foto nel museo?
Pos-soh fah-reh fo-toh nel moo-zeh-oh?

Where can I buy a ticket?
Dove posso comprare un biglietto?
Do-veh pos-soh kom-prah-reh oon beel-yet-toh?

Do I need to book in advance?
Devo prenotare in anticipo?
Deh-voh preh-noh-tah-reh in an-tee-chee-poh?

Is there an audio guide available?
C'è una guida audio disponibile?
Cheh oo-nah gwee-dah ow-dee-oh dee-spon-ee-bee-leh?

How long does the tour take?
Quanto dura il tour?
Kwan-toh doo-rah eel toor?

Are there any temporary exhibitions?
Ci sono mostre temporanee?
Chee soh-noh mos-treh tem-poh-rah-neh?

Where is the museum café?
Dove è il caffè del museo?
Do-veh eh eel kahf-feh del moo-zeh-oh?

Can I enter the museum with a backpack?
Posso entrare nel museo con uno zaino?
Pos-soh en-trah-reh nel moo-zeh-oh kon oo-noh dzah-ee-noh?

Is it allowed to take pictures inside?
È permesso fare fotografie all'interno?
Eh per-mes-soh fah-reh fo-toh-grah-fee al-leen-tehr-noh?

Do you offer guided tours?
Offrite visite guidate?
Of-free-teh vee-zee-teh gwee-dah-teh?

Where can I find the museum map?
Dove posso trovare la mappa del museo?
Do-veh pos-soh troh-vah-reh lah mahp-pah del moo-zeh-oh?

Is the museum accessible for wheelchairs?
Il museo è accessibile per le sedie a rotelle?
Eel moo-zeh-oh eh ak-ches-see-bee-leh pehr leh seh-dee-eh ah roh-tel-leh?

Are pets allowed in the museum?
Gli animali sono ammessi nel museo?
Glee ah-nee-mah-lee soh-noh ahm-mes-see nel moo-zeh-oh?

How much is the entrance fee?
Quanto è il costo d'ingresso?
Kwan-toh eh eel kohs-toh deen-gres-soh?

Where are the restrooms located?

Dove si trovano i bagni?

Do-veh see troh-vah-noh ee bah-nyee?

Can I leave my coat in the cloakroom?

Posso lasciare il mio cappotto in guardaroba?

Pos-soh lah-shee-ah-reh eel mee-oh kap-pot-toh in gwar-dah-roh-bah?

Is there a museum shop?

C'è un negozio del museo?

Cheh oon neh-goh-tsyoh del moo-zeh-oh?

Do you have audio guides in other languages?

Avete guide audio in altre lingue?

Ah-veh-teh gwee-deh ow-dee-oh in ahl-treh leen-gweh?

Music and Books

Where can I buy books?
Dove posso comprare libri?
Do-veh pohs-soh kom-prah-reh lee-bree?

Do you have any recommendations for local music?
Hai qualche consiglio sulla musica locale?
Ahy kwahl-keh kon-see-lyoh soo-lah moo-zee-kah loh-kah-leh?

Can I borrow a book from the library?
Posso prendere in prestito un libro dalla biblioteca?
Pohs-soh prehn-deh-reh een preh-stee-toh oon lee-broh dah-lah bee-blee-oh-teh-kah?

Is there a bookstore nearby?
C'è una libreria qui vicino?
Cheh oo-nah lee-breh-ree-ah kwee vee-chee-noh?

How do I download music?
Come faccio a scaricare musica?
Koh-meh fah-choh ah skah-ree-kah-reh moo-zee-kah?

Where can I find sheet music?
Dove posso trovare spartiti musicali?
Do-veh pohs-soh troh-vah-reh spar-tee-tee moo-zee-kah-lee?

Can I listen to this album before buying?
Posso ascoltare questo album prima di acquistarlo?
Pohs-soh ah-skohl-tah-reh kwes-toh al-boom pree-mah dee ah-kwee-star-loh?

Do you sell vinyl records?
Vendete dischi in vinile?
Ven-deh-teh dees-kee een vee-nee-leh?

Where is the music section?
Dove è la sezione musicale?
Do-veh eh lah seh-tsyoh-neh moo-zee-kah-leh?

Do you have any books in English?
Avete libri in inglese?
Ah-veh-teh lee-bree een een-gleh-seh?

I'm looking for a book about Italian culture.
Cerco un libro sulla cultura italiana.
Chair-koh oon lee-broh soo-lah kool-too-rah ee-tah-lee-ah-nah.

Do you have any classical music CDs?
Avete CD di musica classica?
Ah-veh-teh chee dee dee moo-zee-kah klahs-see-kah?

I need a guitar pick.
Mi serve un plettro per chitarra.
Mee sehr-veh oon pleh-troh pehr kee-tahr-rah.

Can you recommend a good novel?
Puoi consigliarmi un buon romanzo?
Pwoh-ee kon-see-lyahr-mee oon bwon roh-mahn-tsoh?

Where can I find a biography?
Dove posso trovare una biografia?
Do-veh pohs-soh troh-vah-reh oo-nah bee-oh-grah-fee-ah?

Is there a section for travel books?
C'è una sezione per i libri di viaggio?

Cheh oo-nah seh-tsyoh-neh pehr ee lee-bree dee vee-ahj-joh?

Do you have maps and travel guides?
Avete mappe e guide di viaggio?
Ah-veh-teh mahp-peh eh gwee-deh dee vee-ahj-joh?

I'd like to buy a book as a gift.
Vorrei comprare un libro come regalo.
Vohr-ray kom-prah-reh oon lee-broh koh-meh reh-gah-loh.

Can you suggest a good music album for a gift?
Puoi suggerire un buon album musicale per un regalo?
Pwoh-ee soo-jeh-ree-reh oon bwon al-boom moo-zee-kah-leh pehr oon reh-gah-loh?

Where can I charge my e-reader?
Dove posso caricare il mio e-reader?
Doh-veh pohs-soh kah-ree-kah-reh eel mee-oh e-reader

Nightclub

What time does the nightclub open?
Dove apre la discoteca?
Do-veh ah-preh lah dees-koh-teh-kah?

Is there a cover charge?
C'è una tariffa d'ingresso?
Cheh oo-nah tah-ree-fah deen-greh-soh?

Do I need to be on a guest list to enter?
Devo essere su una lista degli invitati per entrare?
Deh-voh eh-seh-reh soo oo-nah lee-stah dehl-lee een-vee-tah-tee pehr en-trah-reh?

What kind of music do you play?
Che tipo di musica suonate?
Keh tee-poh dee moo-see-kah swo-nah-teh?

Do you have a coat check?
Avete un guardaroba?
Ah-veh-teh oon goo-ar-dah-roh-bah?

Is the nightclub accessible for people with disabilities?
La discoteca è accessibile per persone con disabilità?
Lah dees-koh-teh-kah eh ahk-ches-see-bee-leh pehr pehr-soh-neh kohn dee-sah-bee-lee-tah?

Are drinks included in the entrance fee?
Le bevande sono incluse nel prezzo d'ingresso?
Leh beh-vahn-deh soh-noh een-kloo-seh nehl preht-soh deen-greh-soh?

Can I request a song?
Posso richiedere una canzone?
Pohs-soh ree-k'yeh-deh-reh oo-nah kahn-tsoh-neh?

What's the dress code?
Qual è il codice di abbigliamento?
Kwah-leh eel koh-dee-cheh dee ahb-bee-glee-ah-men-toh?

How late is the nightclub open?
Fino a che ora resta aperta la discoteca?
Fee-noh ah keh oh-rah reh-stah ah-pehr-tah lah dees-koh-teh-kah?

Is there a VIP area?
C'è una zona VIP?
Cheh oo-nah tsoh-nah VIP?

Can I pay with a credit card?
Posso pagare con carta di credito?
Pohs-soh pah-gah-reh kohn kahr-tah dee kre-dee-toh?

Do you serve food?
Servite cibo?
Sehr-vee-teh chee-boh?

Are there any special events tonight?
Ci sono eventi speciali stasera?
Chee soh-noh eh-vehn-tee speh-chah-lee stah-seh-rah?

How can I reserve a table?
Come posso prenotare un tavolo?
Koh-meh pohs-soh preh-noh-tah-reh oon tah-voh-loh?

Is there a smoking area?
C'è una zona fumatori?
Cheh oo-nah tsoh-nah foo-mah-toh-ree?

What time does the music start?
A che ora inizia la musica?
Ah keh oh-rah een-ee-tsee-ah lah moo-see-kah?

Can we dance here?
Possiamo ballare qui?
Pohs-see-ah-moh bahl-lah-reh kwee?

Do you have live music?
Avete musica dal vivo?
Ah-veh-teh moo-see-kah dahl vee-voh?

Where can I find the schedule of events?
Dove posso trovare il programma degli eventi?
Do-veh pohs-soh troh-vah-reh eel proh-grahm-mah dehl-lee eh-vehn-tee?

Optician and Ophthalmologist

Do you sell prescription glasses?
Vendete occhiali da vista?
Ven-de-te ok-kee-ah-lee dah vees-tah?

Can I get an eye test here?
Posso fare un test della vista qui?
Pohs-so fah-re oon test del-lah vees-tah kwee?

How much does an eye exam cost?
Quanto costa un esame della vista?
Kwahn-toh koh-stah oon eh-sah-meh del-lah vees-tah?

Do you have sunglasses?
Avete occhiali da sole?
Ah-ve-te ok-kee-ah-lee dah soh-leh?

Can these glasses be ready today?
Questi occhiali possono essere pronti oggi?
Kwes-tee ok-kee-ah-lee pohs-so-no es-se-re prawn-tee ohd-jee?

Do you offer lens replacement service?
Offrite un servizio di sostituzione lenti?
Ohf-free-te oon ser-vee-tsyoh dee soh-stee-too-tsyoh-neh len-tee?

Are these frames made of titanium?
Queste montature sono di titanio?
Kwes-te mon-tah-too-re soh-no dee tee-tah-nee-oh?

How long will the repairs take?
Quanto tempo ci vorrà per le riparazioni?
Kwahn-toh tem-poh chee vohr-rah pehr leh ree-pah-rah-tsyoh-nee?

Do you accept credit cards?
Accettate carte di credito?
Ah-chet-tah-te kar-teh dee kreh-dee-toh?

Is there a warranty on these glasses?
C'è una garanzia su questi occhiali?
Cheh oon-ah gah-ran-tsee-ah soo kwes-tee ok-kee-ah-lee?

Do you have any deals on contact lenses?
Avete offerte su lenti a contatto?
Ah-ve-te ohf-fehr-teh soo len-tee ah kon-tah-toh?

Can I order custom lenses here?
Posso ordinare lenti personalizzate qui?
Pohs-so ohr-dee-nah-re len-tee per-soh-nah-lee-tsa-teh kwee?

Do you provide adjustments for glasses?
Fornite regolazioni per gli occhiali?
For-nee-te reh-goh-lah-tsyoh-nee pehr llee ok-kee-ah-lee?

Can I return these glasses if they don't fit?
Posso restituire questi occhiali se non vanno bene?
Pohs-so reh-stee-too-ee-re kwes-tee ok-kee-ah-lee seh non vahn-no beh-neh?

How do I care for my lenses?
Come devo curare le mie lenti?
Koh-meh deh-voh koo-rah-re leh mee-eh len-tee?

Are there polarized lenses available?
Ci sono lenti polarizzate disponibili?
Chee soh-no len-tee poh-lah-ree-tsa-teh dee-spo-nee-bee-lee?

Do you sell lens cleaning solutions?
Vendete soluzioni per la pulizia delle lenti?
Ven-de-te soh-loo-tsyoh-nee pehr lah poo-lee-tsyah del-leh len-tee?

Can I have my prescription updated here?
Posso aggiornare la mia prescrizione qui?
Pohs-so ah-djohr-nah-re lah mee-ah preh-skree-tsyoh-neh kwee?

Do these lenses protect against UV rays?
Queste lenti proteggono dai raggi UV?
Kwes-te len-tee proh-tehg-go-no dah-ee rahd-jee oo-voo?

How soon can I collect my glasses?
Quando posso ritirare i miei occhiali?
*Kwahn-doh pohs-so ree-tee-rah-re ee mee-eh ok-kee-ah-lee?

Parking and Road Signs

Parking
Parcheggio
Par-kehj-joh

No Parking
Divieto di sosta
Dee-vyeh-toh dee soh-stah

Parking Lot
Parcheggio
Par-kehj-joh

Parking Meter
Parcometro
Par-koh-meh-troh

Disabled Parking
Parcheggio riservato ai disabili
Par-kehj-joh ree-zehr-vah-toh ah-ee dee-zah-bee-lee

Parking Garage
Autorimessa
Ow-toh-ree-mes-sah

Road Sign
Segnale stradale
Sehn-yah-leh strah-dah-leh

Stop Sign
Segnale di stop
Sehn-yah-leh dee stop

Yield

Dare precedenza
Dah-reh preh-cheh-den-tsah

No Entry
Divieto di accesso
Dee-vyeh-toh dee ahk-chess-soh

Speed Limit
Limite di velocità
Lee-mee-teh dee veh-loh-chee-tah

One Way
Senso unico
Sehn-soh oo-nee-koh

Detour
Deviazione
Deh-vyah-tsyoh-neh

Under Construction
Lavori in corso
Lah-voh-ree een kohr-soh

Exit
Uscita
Oo-shee-tah

Entrance
Entrata
Ehn-trah-tah

Pedestrian Crossing
Attraversamento pedonale
At-trah-ver-sah-men-toh peh-doh-nah-leh

Roundabout
Rotonda
Roh-ton-dah

Traffic Lights
Semaforo
Seh-mah-foh-roh

Crossroad
Incrocio
Een-kroh-choh

Peanut Allergies

Does this dish contain peanuts?
Contiene arachidi questo piatto?
Kohn-tyeh-neh ah-rah-kee-dee kweh-stoh pyah-toh?

Can you make it without peanuts?
Puoi farlo senza arachidi?
Pwoh-ee fahr-loh sehn-zah ah-rah-kee-dee?

I'm allergic to peanuts.
Sono allergico alle arachidi.
Soh-noh ahl-lehr-jee-koh ahl-leh ah-rah-kee-dee.

Is there peanut oil in this?
C'è olio di arachidi in questo?
Cheh oh-lyoh dee ah-rah-kee-dee een kweh-stoh?

Could you check the ingredients for peanuts?
Potresti controllare gli ingredienti per le arachidi?
Poh-treh-stee kohn-trohl-lah-reh lyee een-greh-dyehn-tee pehr leh ah-rah-kee-dee?

What alternatives do you have that are peanut-free?
Quali alternative hai che sono senza arachidi?
Kwah-lee ahl-tehr-nah-tee-veh ah-ee keh soh-noh sehn-zah ah-rah-kee-dee?

Do you use peanut products in your kitchen?
Usi prodotti di arachidi nella tua cucina?
Oo-zee proh-doh-tee dee ah-rah-kee-dee nehl-lah too-ah koo-chee-nah?

I need a dish that has no peanuts.
Ho bisogno di un piatto che non abbia arachidi.
Oh bee-zoh-nyoh dee oon pyah-toh keh nohn ahb-byah ah-rah-kee-dee.

Can I see the allergy information?
Posso vedere le informazioni sulle allergie?
Pohs-soh veh-deh-reh leh een-fohr-mah-tsyoh-nee sool-leh ahl-lehr-jee-eh?

Is this meal safe for someone with a peanut allergy?
Questo pasto è sicuro per qualcuno con allergia alle arachidi?
Kweh-stoh pahs-toh eh see-koo-roh pehr kwahl-koo-noh kohn ahl-lehr-jee-ah ahl-leh ah-rah-kee-dee?

Are there any peanut traces in this?
Ci sono tracce di arachidi in questo?
Chee soh-noh trah-cheh dee ah-rah-kee-dee een kweh-stoh?

How do you prevent cross-contamination with peanuts?
Come prevenite la contaminazione incrociata con le arachidi?
Koh-meh preh-veh-nee-teh lah kohn-tah-mee-nah-tsyoh-neh een-kroh-chah-tah kohn leh ah-rah-kee-dee?

Can you recommend a peanut-free dish?
Puoi consigliare un piatto senza arachidi?
Pwoh-ee kohn-see-lyah-reh oon pyah-toh sehn-zah ah-rah-kee-dee?

Do you have a separate area for cooking peanut-free meals?
Avete un'area separata per cucinare pasti senza arachidi?
Ah-veh-teh oon'ah-reh-ah sehp-ah-rah-tah pehr koo-chee-nah-reh pah-stee sehn-zah ah-rah-kee-dee?

Is the dessert menu peanut-free?
Il menu dei dolci è senza arachidi?
Eel meh-noo dey dohl-chee eh sehn-zah ah-rah-kee-dee?

Are your sauces peanut-free?
Le tue salse sono senza arachidi?
Leh too-eh sahl-seh soh-noh sehn-zah ah-rah-kee-dee?

Do any of your dishes use peanut butter?
Qualcuno dei tuoi piatti usa il burro di arachidi?
Kwahl-koo-noh dey too-ee pyah-tee oo-zah eel boor-roh dee ah-rah-kee-dee?

I must avoid peanuts, can you help?
Devo evitare le arachidi, puoi aiutarmi?
Deh-voh eh-vee-tah-reh leh ah-rah-kee-dee, pwoh-ee ah-yoo-tahr-mee?

Are the breads made without peanut products?
I pani sono fatti senza prodotti di arachidi?
Ee pah-nee soh-noh fah-tee sehn-zah proh-doh-tee dee ah-rah-kee-dee?

Is there anything peanut-free I can snack on?
C'è qualcosa senza arachidi che posso sgranocchiare?
Cheh kwahl-koh-sah sehn-zah ah-rah-kee-dee keh pohs-soh sgahn-nohk-kyah-reh?

Pharmacy

Where is the nearest pharmacy?
Dove è la farmacia più vicina?
Do-veh eh lah far-mah-chee-ah pyoo vee-chee-noh?

I need pain relievers.
Ho bisogno di antidolorifici.
Oh bee-zoh-nyoh dee an-tee-doh-loh-ree-fee-chee.

Do you have something for a cold?
Avete qualcosa per il raffreddore?
Ah-veh-teh kwahl-koh-sah pehr eel rahf-freh-doh-reh?

I need allergy medication.
Ho bisogno di farmaci per le allergie.
Oh bee-zoh-nyoh dee far-mah-chee pehr leh al-ler-jee.

Can I buy band-aids here?
Posso comprare cerotti qui?
Pohs-soh kom-prah-reh cheh-roh-tee kwee?

I'm looking for sunscreen.
Cerco una crema solare.
Chair-koh oo-nah kreh-mah soh-lah-reh.

Do you have insect repellent?
Avete un repellente per insetti?
Ah-veh-teh oon reh-pel-len-teh pehr een-seht-tee?

I need a thermometer.
Ho bisogno di un termometro.
Oh bee-zoh-nyoh dee oon tehr-moh-meh-troh.

Is this medicine available without a prescription?
Questo farmaco è disponibile senza ricetta?
Kwes-toh far-mah-koh eh dee-spo-nee-bee-leh sehn-zah ree-cheh-tah?

I need something for an upset stomach.
Ho bisogno di qualcosa per lo stomaco disturbato.
Oh bee-zoh-nyoh dee kwahl-koh-sah pehr loh sto-mah-koh dee-stoor-bah-toh.

Where can I get first aid?
Dove posso ricevere i primi soccorsi?
Do-veh pohs-soh ree-cheh-veh-reh ee pree-mee soh-kohr-see?

I have a fever.
Ho la febbre.
Oh lah fehb-breh.

I need cough syrup.
Ho bisogno di sciroppo per la tosse.
Oh bee-zoh-nyoh dee shee-rohp-poh pehr lah tos-seh.

Can you recommend a remedy for burns?
Puoi consigliare un rimedio per le ustioni?
Pwoh-ee kon-see-lyah-reh oon ree-meh-dyoh pehr leh oos-tyoh-nee?

Do you sell diabetic supplies?
Vendete forniture per diabetici?
Ven-deh-teh for-nee-too-reh pehr dyah-beh-tee-chee?

I'm looking for vitamins.
Cerco vitamine.
Chair-koh vee-tah-mee-neh.

Do you have lactose-free products?
Avete prodotti senza lattosio?
Ah-veh-teh proh-doh-tee sehn-zah laht-toh-syoh?

I need a prescription refill.
Ho bisogno di una ricarica della ricetta.
Oh bee-zoh-nyoh dee oo-nah ree-kah-ree-kah del-lah ree-cheh-tah.

Do you have herbal teas?
Avete tisane?
Ah-veh-teh tee-zah-neh?

I need a plaster for a sprain.
Ho bisogno di un cerotto per una distorsione.
Oh bee-zoh-nyoh dee oon cheh-roh-toh pehr oo-nah dee-stohr-syoh-neh.

Pharmacy
Farmacia
Far-mah-chee-ah

Prescription
Ricetta
Ree-chet-tah

Painkiller
Analgesico
Ah-nahl-jeh-see-koh

Antibiotic
Antibiotico
An-tee-byoh-tee-koh

Band-Aid
Cerotto
Cheh-roht-toh

First Aid Kit
Kit di pronto soccorso
Keet dee prohn-toh soh-kohr-soh

Cough Syrup
Sciroppo per la tosse
Shee-rohp-poh pehr lah tohs-seh

Sunscreen
Crema solare
Kreh-mah soh-lah-reh

Allergy Medication
Farmaco per allergie
Far-mah-koh pehr al-lehr-jee-eh

Thermometer
Termometro
Ter-moh-meh-troh

Antiseptic
Antisettico
An-tee-seh-tee-koh

Inhaler
Inhalatore
Ee-nah-lah-toh-reh

Vitamins
Vitamine
Vee-tah-mee-neh

Eye Drops
Collirio
Kohl-lee-ree-oh

Motion Sickness Pills
Pillole per il mal di movimento
Pee-loh-leh pehr eel mahl dee moh-vee-men-toh

Antifungal Cream
Crema antifungina
Kreh-mah an-tee-foon-jee-nah

Diarrhea Medicine
Medicina per la diarrea
Meh-dee-chee-nah pehr lah dee-ah-reh-ah

Blood Pressure Monitor
Misuratore di pressione
Mee-soo-rah-toh-reh dee preh-ssyo-neh

Nasal Spray
Spray nasale
Sprahy nah-sah-leh

Contraceptives
Contraccettivi
Kon-trah-chet-tee-vee

Phrases for Daily Use

Hello! / Goodbye!
Ciao! / Arrivederci!
Chah-oh! / Ah-ree-veh-dehr-chee!

Please.
Per favore.
Pehr fah-voh-reh.

Thank you.
Grazie.
Grah-tsyeh.

Excuse me.
Scusi.
Skoo-zee.

Yes. / No.
Sì. / No.
See. / Noh.

I do not understand.
Non capisco.
Nohn kah-pee-skoh.

Can you help me?
Può aiutarmi?
Pwoh ah-yoo-tahr-mee?

How much does it cost?
Quanto costa?
Kwan-toh koh-stah?

Where is...?
Dove è...?
Doh-veh eh...?

I would like...
Vorrei...
Vohr-ray...

I'm looking for...
Sto cercando...
Stoh cher-kahn-doh...

Do you speak English?
Parla inglese?
Pahr-lah een-gleh-seh?

I need...
Ho bisogno di...
Oh bee-zoh-nyoh dee...

I'm allergic to...
Sono allergico/a a...
Soh-noh ah-lleh-ree-koh/ah ah...

Can I have the bill, please?
Posso avere il conto, per favore?
Pohs-soh ah-veh-reh eel kohn-toh, pehr fah-voh-reh?

Can I use your phone?
Posso usare il tuo telefono?
Pohs-soh oo-zah-reh eel twoh teh-leh-foh-noh?

Social Conversations

How are you?
Come stai?
Koh-meh stai?

What's your name?
Come ti chiami?
Koh-meh tee kee-ah-mee?

Where are you from?
Di dove sei?
Dee doh-veh seh-ee?

Do you speak English?
Parli inglese?
Pahr-lee een-gleh-seh?

I'm here on vacation.
Sono qui in vacanza.
Soh-noh kwee een vah-kahn-tsah.

What do you recommend visiting in this city?
Cosa consigli di visitare in questa città?
Koh-sah kohn-see-lyee dee vee-zee-tah-reh een kweh-stah chee-tah?

Can we take a photo together?
Possiamo fare una foto insieme?
Poh-see-ah-moh fah-reh oo-nah foh-toh een-see-eh-meh?

What's your favorite food?
Qual è il tuo cibo preferito?
Kwah-leh eel too-oh chee-boh preh-feh-ree-toh?

Do you know a good place to eat here?
Conosci un buon posto dove mangiare qui?
Kohn-soh-shee oon bwon poh-stoh doh-veh mahn-jah-reh kwee?

What do you like to do in your free time?
Cosa ti piace fare nel tempo libero?
Koh-sah tee pee-ah-cheh fah-reh nehl tehm-poh lee-beh-roh?

How long have you been living here?
Da quanto tempo vivi qui?
Dah kwahn-toh tehm-poh vee-vee kwee?

Can you show me on the map?
Puoi mostrarmi sulla mappa?
Pwoh-ee moh-strahr-mee soo-lah mahp-pah?

I love this city!
Adoro questa città!
Ah-doh-roh kweh-stah chee-tah!

It's nice to meet you.
È un piacere conoscerti.
Eh oon pyah-cheh-reh koh-noh-shehr-tee.

Could you help me, please?
Potresti aiutarmi, per favore?
Poh-trehs-tee ah-yoo-tahr-mee, pehr fah-voh-reh?

What are the local customs?
Quali sono le usanze locali?
Kwah-lee soh-noh leh oo-sahn-tseh loh-kah-lee?

I'm looking for the museum.
Sto cercando il museo.
Stoh chehr-kahn-doh eel moo-seh-oh.

Where can I buy souvenirs?

Dove posso comprare souvenir?

Doh-veh pohs-soh kohm-prah-reh soo-veh-neer?

Can I try this, please?

Posso provare questo, per favore?

Pohs-soh proh-vah-reh kweh-stoh, pehr fah-voh-reh?

I would like to make a reservation.

Vorrei fare una prenotazione.

Vohr-reh-ee fah-reh oo-nah preh-noh-tah-tsyoh-neh.

Phrases You Can Use to Start a Conversation

What's your name?
Come ti chiami?
Ko-meh tee kyah-mee?

What's your favorite local dish?
Qual è il tuo piatto locale preferito?
Kwah-leh eel too-oh pyah-toh loh-kah-leh preh-feh-ree-toh?

How long have you lived in this city?
Da quanto tempo vivi in questa città?
Dah kwahn-toh tem-poh vee-vee een kwes-tah chee-tah?

What's the best place to visit in this city?
Qual è il miglior posto da visitare in questa città?
Kwah-leh eel meel-yohr poh-stoh dah vee-zee-tah-reh een kwes-tah chee-tah?

Can you tell me more about this neighborhood?
Puoi dirmi di più su questo quartiere?
Pwoh-ee deermee dee pyoo soo kwes-toh kwahr-tee-eh-reh?

Where can I find the best coffee in town?
Dove posso trovare il miglior caffè della città?
Do-veh pohs-soh troh-vah-reh eel meel-yohr kahf-feh del-lah chee-tah?

Are there any hidden gems in this city?
Ci sono gioielli nascosti in questa città?
Chee soh-noh joh-yehl-lee nahs-koh-stee een kwes-tah chee-tah?

What's the most interesting historical site here?
Qual è il sito storico più interessante qui?
Kwah-leh eel see-toh stoh-ree-koh pyoo een-teh-reh-sahn-teh kwee?

Can you suggest a quiet place to relax?
Puoi suggerire un posto tranquillo per rilassarsi?
Pwoh-ee sooj-jeh-ree-reh oon poh-stoh trahn-kweel-loh pehr ree-lah-sahr-see?

Where's the best place to watch the sunset?
Dove è il miglior posto per guardare il tramonto?
Do-veh eh eel meel-yohr poh-stoh pehr gwahr-dah-reh eel trah-mon-toh?

Do you know where I can rent a bike?
Sai dove posso noleggiare una bicicletta?
Sah-ee do-veh pohs-soh noh-leh-jah-reh oo-nah bee-chee-klet-tah?

What festivals do you recommend in this area?
Quali festival consigli in questa zona?
Kwah-lee fes-tee-vahl kon-see-lyee een kwes-tah zoh-nah?

Is there a local market you would recommend?
C'è un mercato locale che consiglieresti?
Cheh oon mehr-kah-toh loh-kah-leh keh kon-see-lyeh-rehs-tee?

Where can I try the best local wine?
Dove posso provare il miglior vino locale?
Do-veh pohs-soh proh-vah-reh eel meel-yohr vee-noh loh-kah-leh?

Can you help me with directions to this place?
Puoi aiutarmi con le direzioni per questo posto?
Pwoh-ee ah-yoo-tahr-mee kon leh dee-reh-tsyoh-nee pehr kwes-toh poh-stoh?

What is the local specialty here?
Qual è la specialità locale qui?
Kwah-leh lah speh-chah-lee-tah loh-kah-leh kwee?

What's your favorite part of the city?
Qual è la tua parte preferita della città?
Kwah-leh lah too-ah par-teh preh-feh-ree-tah dehl-lah chee-tah?

Can you recommend a good restaurant around here?
Puoi consigliare un buon ristorante qui vicino?
Pwoh-ee kohn-see-lyah-reh oon bwon ree-stoh-rahn-teh kwee vee-chee-noh?

Do you know where I can find a good coffee?
Sai dove posso trovare un buon caffè?
Sah-ee doh-veh pohs-soh troh-vah-reh oon bwon kaf-feh?

What's a traditional dish I should try?
Qual è un piatto tradizionale che dovrei provare?
Kwah-leh oon pyah-toh trah-dee-tsyoh-nah-leh keh doh-vreh-ee proh-vah-reh?

Do you enjoy living in this city?
Ti piace vivere in questa città?
Tee pyah-cheh vee-veh-reh een kweh-stah chee-tah?

Where's a good place to see the sunset?
Dove è un buon posto per vedere il tramonto?
Do-veh eh oon bwon pohs-toh pehr veh-deh-reh eel trah-mon-toh?

Can you suggest a nice place for a walk?
Puoi suggerire un bel posto per una passeggiata?
Pwoh-ee sooj-jeh-ree-reh oon behl pohs-toh pehr oo-nah pahs-sej-jee-ah-tah?

What do you like to do in your free time?
Cosa ti piace fare nel tuo tempo libero?
Koh-sah tee pyah-cheh fah-reh nehl too-oh tem-poh lee-beh-roh?

Where can I buy souvenirs?
Dove posso comprare souvenir?
Do-veh pohs-soh kom-prah-reh soo-veh-neer?

Do you have any plans for tonight?
Hai dei piani per stasera?
Ah-ee deh-ee pyah-nee pehr stah-seh-rah?

How long have you lived here?
Da quanto tempo vivi qui?
Dah kwahn-toh tem-poh vee-vee kwee?

What should I definitely see in this city?
Cosa dovrei assolutamente vedere in questa città?
Koh-sah doh-vreh-ee as-soh-loo-tah-men-teh veh-deh-reh een kweh-stah chee-tah?

Where's the best place to relax in the city?
Dove è il posto migliore per rilassarsi in città?
Do-veh eh eel pohs-toh meel-yoh-reh pehr ree-lahs-sahr-see een chee-tah?

Can you tell me more about this area?
Puoi dirmi di più su questa zona?
Pwoh-ee deermee dee pyoo soo kweh-stah tsoh-nah?

Are there any festivals happening soon?
Ci sono festival in arrivo?
Chee soh-noh fehs-tee-vahl een ah-ree-voh?

What's the best way to get around the city?
Qual è il modo migliore per muoversi in città?
*Kwah-leh eel moh-doh meel-yoh-reh pehr mwoh-vehr-see
een chee-tah?*

What's the history behind this place?
Qual è la storia dietro questo posto?
Kwah-leh lah stoh-ree-ah dee-eh-troh kweh-stoh pohs-toh?

Do you come here often?
Dove vieni qui spesso?
Do-veh vye-nee kwee speh-soh?

Have you tried the coffee here?
Hai provato il caffè qui?
Eye proh-vah-toh eel kaf-feh kwee?

What do you recommend from the menu?
Cosa consigli del menu?
Koh-sah kohn-see-lyee del meh-noo?

What's your favorite book?
Qual è il tuo libro preferito?
Kwal eh eel too-oh lee-broh preh-feh-ree-toh?

Do you like to travel?
Ti piace viaggiare?
Tee pyah-che vee-ah-jah-reh?

Have you been to any interesting places recently?
Sei stato in posti interessanti di recente?
Say stah-toh een poh-stee een-teh-reh-sahn-tee dee reh-chehn-teh?

What kind of music do you like?
Che tipo di musica ti piace?
Keh tee-poh dee moo-see-kah tee pyah-che?

Do you have any hobbies?
Hai qualche hobby?
Eye kwal-kweh ob-bee?

What do you do for fun?
Cosa fai per divertirti?
Koh-sah fye per dee-ver-teer-tee?

Are you interested in art?
Ti interessa l'arte?
Tee een-teh-reh-sah lar-teh?

Do you watch any sports?
Guardi qualche sport?
Gwar-dee kwal-kweh spor-t?

What brings you here today?
Cosa ti porta qui oggi?
Koh-sah tee por-tah kwee ohd-jee?

Have you ever been to Italy?
Sei mai stato in Italia?
Say my stah-toh een Ee-tah-lyah?

What's your favorite movie?
Qual è il tuo film preferito?
Kwal eh eel too-oh feelm preh-feh-ree-toh?

What's your idea of a perfect day?
Qual è la tua idea di una giornata perfetta?
Kwal eh lah too-ah ee-dee-ah dee oo-nah jor-nah-tah per-feh-tah?

Do you enjoy cooking?
Ti piace cucinare?
Tee pyah-che koo-chee-nah-reh?

What are you drinking?
Cosa stai bevendo?
Ko-zah sty beh-ven-doh?

This place has a great vibe, don't you think?
Questo posto ha un'ottima atmosfera, non credi?
Kweh-stoh poh-stoh ah oon-ot-tee-mah ah-toh-sfeh-rah, non kreh-dee?

Can I buy you a drink?
Posso offrirti da bere?
Pohs-soh of-feer-tee dah beh-reh?

What's your favorite drink?
Qual è la tua bevanda preferita?
Kwah-l eh lah too-ah beh-vahn-dah preh-feh-ree-tah?

Have you tried the food here?
Hai provato il cibo qui?
Ay proh-vah-toh eel chee-boh kwee?

What music do you like?
Che musica ti piace?
Ke moo-see-kah tee pyah-cheh?

Are you from around here?
Sei di queste parti?
Sey dee kweh-steh par-tee?

Do you have any recommendations for a good book?
Hai qualche consiglio per un buon libro?
Ay kwal-keh kon-see-lyoh pehr oon bwon lee-broh?

How do you spend your free time?
Come trascorri il tuo tempo libero?
Ko-meh tra-skor-ree eel too-oh tem-poh lee-beh-roh?

I love this song, do you?
Adoro questa canzone, e tu?
Ah-doh-roh kweh-stah kan-tsoh-neh, eh too?

What brings you here today?
Cosa ti porta qui oggi?
Ko-zah tee pohr-tah kwee ohd-jee?

Have you been here before?
Sei mai stato qui prima?
Sey my stah-toh kwee pree-mah?

Do you like to travel?
Ti piace viaggiare?
Tee pyah-cheh vyah-djah-reh?

Do you know any good places to eat around here?
Conosci posti buoni dove mangiare qui vicino?
Kohn-noh-shee poh-stee bwon-ee doh-veh mahn-djah-reh kwee vee-chee-noh?

What do you do for work?
Che lavoro fai?
Ke lah-voh-roh fy?

Have you seen any good movies recently?
Hai visto qualche film interessante di recente?
Ay vees-toh kwal-keh feelm een-teh-res-san-teh dee reh-chen-teh?

Police and Carabinieri

Can you call the police for me?
Puoi chiamare la polizia per me?
Pwoh-ee kee-ah-mah-reh lah poh-lee-tsee-ah pehr meh?

Is this the number for emergencies?
È questo il numero per le emergenze?
Eh kweh-stoh eel noo-meh-roh pehr leh eh-mehr-dzehn-tseh?

Where is the nearest police station?
Dove è la stazione di polizia più vicina?
Do-veh eh lah stah-tsee-oh-neh dee poh-lee-tsee-ah pyoo vee-chee-nah?

How do I report a theft?
Come faccio a denunciare un furto?
Koh-meh fah-cho ah deh-noon-tshee-ah-reh oon foor-toh?

Can I have the police department's phone number?
Posso avere il numero di telefono del dipartimento di polizia?
Pohs-soh ah-veh-reh eel noo-meh-roh dee teh-leh-foh-noh dehl dee-pahr-tee-men-toh dee poh-lee-tsee-ah?

What should I do if I lose my passport?
Cosa dovrei fare se perdo il mio passaporto?
Koh-sah doh-vreh-ee fah-reh seh pehr-doh eel mee-oh pahs-sah-pohr-toh?

Are there any police officers nearby?
Ci sono agenti di polizia nelle vicinanze?
Chee soh-noh ah-dzhen-tee dee poh-lee-tsee-ah neh-lleh vee-chee-nahn-tseh?

How can I get to the Carabinieri station?
Come posso arrivare alla stazione dei Carabinieri?
Koh-meh pohs-soh ah-rree-vah-reh ah-lah stah-tsee-oh-neh deh-ee kah-rah-bee-nyeh-ree?

I need to report a lost item.
Devo denunciare un oggetto perso.
Deh-voh deh-noon-tshee-ah-reh oon oh-dzheht-toh pehr-soh?

Who do I contact for a noise complaint?
Chi devo contattare per una denuncia di rumore?
Kee deh-voh kon-tah-tah-reh pehr oo-nah deh-noon-tsee-ah dee roo-moh-reh?

Is it safe to walk here at night?
È sicuro camminare qui di notte?
Eh see-koo-roh kahm-mee-nah-reh kwee dee noh-teh?

What are the emergency numbers in Italy?
Quali sono i numeri di emergenza in Italia?
Kwah-lee soh-noh ee noo-meh-ree dee eh-mehr-dzehn-tsah een Ee-tah-lyah?

Can you help me find the nearest Carabinieri?
Puoi aiutarmi a trovare i Carabinieri più vicini?
Pwoh-ee ah-yoo-tahr-mee ah troh-vah-reh ee Kah-rah-bee-nyeh-ree pyoo vee-chee-nee?

How do I file a police report?
Come faccio a fare una denuncia alla polizia?
Koh-meh fah-cho ah fah-reh oo-nah deh-noon-tsee-ah ah-lah poh-lee-tsee-ah?

What's the difference between police and Carabinieri?
Qual è la differenza tra polizia e Carabinieri?
Kwah-l eh lah dee-feh-ren-tsah trah poh-lee-tsee-ah eh Kah-rah-bee-nyeh-ree?

Can I talk to an English-speaking officer?
Posso parlare con un agente che parla inglese?
Pohs-soh pahr-lah-reh kon oon ah-dzhen-teh keh pahr-lah een-gleh-seh?

Where can I get legal assistance?
Dove posso ottenere assistenza legale?
Do-veh pohs-soh oh-teh-neh-reh ah-ssees-ten-tsah leh-gah-leh?

I lost my wallet, what should I do?
Ho perso il mio portafoglio, cosa dovrei fare?
Oh pehr-soh eel mee-oh pohr-tah-foh-lyoh, koh-sah doh-vreh-ee fah-reh?

Is there a lost and found at the police station?
C'è un ufficio oggetti smarriti alla stazione di polizia?
Cheh oon oof-fee-tchoh ohd-zhet-tee smahr-ree-tee ah-lah stah-tsee-oh-neh dee poh-lee-tsee-ah?

How do I ask for police protection?
Come chiedo la protezione della polizia?
Koh-meh kee-eh-doh lah proh-teh-tsee-oh-neh dehl-lah poh-lee-tsee-ah?

Post Office

Where is the post office?
Dove è l'ufficio postale?
Do-veh eh eel oof-fee-choh poh-stah-leh?

Can I buy stamps here?
Posso comprare francobolli qui?
Pohs-soh kohm-prah-reh frahn-koh-bohl-lee kwee?

What time does the post office close?
A che ora chiude l'ufficio postale?
Ah keh oh-rah kyoo-deh l'oof-fee-choh poh-stah-leh?

Is there a mailbox nearby?
C'è una cassetta postale nelle vicinanze?
Cheh oo-nah kahs-seh-tah poh-stah-leh nel-leh vee-chee-nahn-tseh?

How do I send a package?
Come faccio a inviare un pacco?
Koh-meh fah-choh ah een-vyah-reh oon pahk-koh?

Do you sell envelopes?
Vendete buste?
Vehn-deh-teh boo-steh?

How much does it cost to send this to the United States?
Quanto costa inviare questo negli Stati Uniti?
Kwahn-toh koh-stah een-vyah-reh kweh-stoh neh-glee Stah-tee Oo-nee-tee?

Can I have some bubble wrap?
Posso avere del pluriball?
Pohs-soh ah-veh-reh del ploo-ree-bahl?

157

Where can I fill out this form?
Dove posso compilare questo modulo?
Do-veh pohs-soh kohm-pee-lah-reh kweh-stoh moh-doo-loh?

Is this the right counter for international shipments?
Questo è lo sportello giusto per le spedizioni internazionali?
Kweh-stoh eh loh spor-tel-loh joo-stoh pehr leh speh-dee-tsee-oh-nee een-ter-nah-tsee-oh-nah-lee?

How long will it take for my parcel to arrive?
Quanto tempo ci vuole per che il mio pacco arrivi?
Kwahn-toh tem-poh chee vwoh-leh pehr keh eel mee-oh pahk-koh ah-ree-vee?

Do I need to sign for it?
Devo firmare?
Deh-voh feer-mah-reh?

Where can I get a tracking number?
Dove posso ottenere un numero di tracciamento?
Do-veh pohs-soh oh-teh-neh-reh oon noo-meh-roh dee trah-chah-men-toh?

Can you weigh this, please?
Puoi pesare questo, per favore?
Pwoh-ee peh-sah-reh kweh-stoh, pehr fah-voh-reh?

What is the weight limit for this package?
Qual è il limite di peso per questo pacco?
Kwah-leh eel lee-mee-teh dee peh-soh pehr kweh-stoh pahk-koh?

Can I ship this as fragile?
Posso spedire questo come fragile?
Pohs-soh speh-dee-reh kweh-stoh koh-meh frah-jee-leh?

Do you have any boxes for sale?
Avete scatole in vendita?
Ah-veh-teh ska-toh-leh een vehn-dee-tah?

How can I insure my shipment?
Come posso assicurare la mia spedizione?
Koh-meh pohs-soh ah-see-koo-rah-reh lah mee-ah speh-dee-tsee-oh-neh?

What forms of payment do you accept?
Quali forme di pagamento accettate?
Kwah-lee for-meh dee pah-gah-men-toh ah-chet-tah-teh?

Is there an express service?
C'è un servizio espresso?
Cheh oon sehr-vee-tsee-oh ehs-preh-soh?

Pub

What beers do you have?
Che birre avete?
Keh bee-rreh ah-veh-teh?

Can I see the menu, please?
Posso vedere il menù, per favore?
Pohs-soh veh-deh-reh eel meh-noo, pehr fah-voh-reh?

Is there any vegetarian option?
C'è qualche opzione vegetariana?
Cheh kwahl-keh ohp-zee-oh-neh veh-geh-tah-ree-ah-nah?

Could I get a glass of water?
Potrei avere un bicchiere d'acqua?
Poh-treh-ee ah-veh-reh oon bee-kkee-eh-reh dahk-kwah?

How much is this beer?
Quanto costa questa birra?
Kwahn-toh koh-stah kweh-stah beer-rah?

Do you accept credit cards?
Accettate carte di credito?
Ah-cheh-tah-teh kahr-teh dee kreh-dee-toh?

Could I have the bill, please?
Potrei avere il conto, per favore?
Poh-treh-ee ah-veh-reh eel kohn-toh, pehr fah-voh-reh?

Is there a table available?
C'è un tavolo disponibile?
Cheh oon tah-voh-loh dee-spoh-nee-bee-leh?

Can I order now?
Posso ordinare ora?
Pohs-soh ohr-dee-nah-reh oh-rah?

Do you have any specials today?
Avete qualche piatto speciale oggi?
Ah-veh-teh kwahl-keh pyah-toh speh-chah-leh ohd-jee?

Can I have a pint, please?
Posso avere una pinta, per favore?
Pohs-soh ah-veh-reh ooh-nah peen-tah, pehr fah-voh-reh?

What's the WiFi password?
Qual è la password del WiFi?
Kwahl eh lah pahss-wohrd dehl Wee-Fee?

Is this beer on tap?
Questa birra è alla spina?
Kweh-stah beer-rah eh ah-lah spee-nah?

Can we sit outside?
Possiamo sederci fuori?
Pohs-see-ah-moh seh-dehr-chee fwoh-ree?

Do you serve food here?
Servite cibo qui?
Sehr-vee-teh chee-boh kwee?

What time do you close?
A che ora chiudete?
Ah keh oh-rah kyoo-deh-teh?

Can I pay separately?
Posso pagare separatamente?
Pohs-soh pah-gah-reh seh-pah-rah-tah-men-teh?

Do you have non-alcoholic drinks?

Avete bevande senza alcol?

Ah-veh-teh beh-vahn-deh sehn-zah ahl-kohl?

How long is the wait?

Quanto è l'attesa?

Kwahn-toh eh laht-teh-sah?

Can I get a refill on this?

Posso avere un ricarico su questo?

Pohs-soh ah-veh-reh oon ree-kah-ree-koh soo kweh-stoh?

Renting a Car

How much does it cost to rent a car?
Quanto costa noleggiare un'auto?
Kwan-to kos-ta no-lej-ja-re oon-ow-to?

Do I need an international driver's license?
Ho bisogno di una patente internazionale?
O bi-zo-ɲo di oo-na pa-ten-te in-ter-na-tsyo-na-le?

Can I return the car in a different location?
Posso restituire l'auto in un'altra località?
Pos-so re-sti-too-i-re low-to in oon-al-tra lo-ka-li-ta?

What is the fuel policy?
Qual è la politica sul carburante?
Kwal e la po-li-ti-ka sol kar-bu-ran-te?

Is insurance included in the rental?
L'assicurazione è inclusa nel noleggio?
Las-si-ku-ra-tsyo-ne e in-kloo-sa nel no-lej-jo?

What do I do in case of an accident?
Cosa devo fare in caso di incidente?
Ko-za de-vo fa-re in ka-zo di in-tsi-den-te?

Can I add an additional driver?
Posso aggiungere un altro guidatore?
Pos-so aj-jun-ge-re oon al-tro gwi-da-to-re?

How can I cancel my reservation?
Come posso cancellare la mia prenotazione?
Ko-me pos-so kan-tʃe-la-re la mi-a pre-no-ta-tsyo-ne?

Do you have automatic cars?
Avete auto automatiche?
A-ve-te ow-to aw-to-ma-ti-ke?

What documents do I need to rent a car?
Quali documenti sono necessari per noleggiare un'auto?
Kwa-li do-ku-men-ti so-no ne-tses-sa-ri per no-lej-ja-re oon-ow-to?

Is there a mileage limit?
C'è un limite di chilometraggio?
Tʃe oon li-mi-te di ki-lo-me-tra-jjo?

Can I pay with a credit card?
Posso pagare con una carta di credito?
Pos-so pa-ga-re kon oo-na kar-ta di kre-di-to?

Do you offer roadside assistance?
Offrite assistenza stradale?
Of-fri-te as-sis-ten-tsa stra-da-le?

Can I rent a GPS with the car?
Posso noleggiare un GPS con l'auto?
Pos-so no-lej-ja-re oon GPS kon low-to?

Are there any additional fees?
Ci sono costi aggiuntivi?
Tʃi so-no kos-ti ad-dʒun-ti-vi?

How old do I have to be to rent a car?
Quanti anni devo avere per noleggiare un'auto?
Kwan-ti an-ni de-vo a-ve-re per no-lej-ja-re oon-ow-to?

Can I rent a car with a debit card?
Posso noleggiare un'auto con una carta di debito?
Pos-so no-lej-ja-re oon-ow-to kon oo-na kar-ta di de-bi-to?

What type of car do you recommend for the city?
Che tipo di auto consigliate per la città?
Ke ti-po di ow-to kon-si-ʎa-te per la tʃit-ta?

Do I need to pay a deposit?
Devo pagare un deposito?
De-vo pa-ga-re oon de-po-si-to?

Can I extend my rental period?
Posso prolungare il periodo di noleggio
Pohs-soh proh-loon-gah-reh eel peh-ree-oh-doh dee noh-leh-joh?

Restaurant

How is this dish prepared?
Come è preparato questo piatto?
Ko-um eh preh-pah-rah-toh kwest-oh pyah-toh?

Does this dish contain gluten?
Questo piatto contiene glutine?
Kwest-oh pyah-toh kon-tyayn-e gloo-tee-nay?

Can I have the menu, please?
Posso avere il menu, per favore?
Pohs-soh ah-veh-ray eel men-oo, pehr fah-voh-ray?

Is there a vegetarian option?
C'è un'opzione vegetariana?
Cheh oon op-tsyoh-nay veh-jeh-tah-ree-ah-nah?

Can I have a glass of water?
Posso avere un bicchiere d'acqua?
Pohs-soh ah-veh-ray oon bee-kee-eh-ray dahk-kwah?

What do you recommend?
Cosa consigli?
Koh-sah kohn-see-lee?

Do you have a table outside?
Avete un tavolo fuori?
Ah-veh-tay oon tah-voh-loh fwoh-ree?

Can I see the wine list?
Posso vedere la lista dei vini?
Pohs-soh veh-deh-ray lah lees-tah day vee-nee?

Are you open on Sundays?
Siete aperti la domenica?
See-eh-tay ah-pehr-tee lah doh-meh-nee-kah?

Can we have some bread?
Possiamo avere del pane?
Pohs-syah-moh ah-veh-ray dehl pah-nay?

Is the tip included?
La mancia è inclusa?
Lah mahn-chah eh een-kloo-sah?

Can I pay by credit card?
Posso pagare con la carta di credito?
Pohs-soh pah-gah-ray kohn lah kahr-tah dee kre-dee-toh?

Do you have any specials today?
Avete piatti speciali oggi?
Ah-veh-tay pyah-tee speh-chah-lee ohd-jee?

I am allergic to peanuts.
Sono allergico alle arachidi.
Soh-noh ah-lleh-ree-jee-koh ah-lleh ah-rah-kee-dee?

Can I have the bill, please?
Posso avere il conto, per favore?
Pohs-soh ah-veh-ray eel kohn-toh, pehr fah-voh-ray?

Do you offer gluten-free options?
Offrite opzioni senza glutine?
Ohf-free-tay op-tsyoh-nee sehn-zah gloo-tee-nay?

Can I make a reservation?
Posso fare una prenotazione?
Pohs-soh fah-ray oon-ah preh-noh-tah-tsyoh-nay?

Is this spicy?

Questo è piccante?

Kwest-oh eh pee-kahn-tay?

Do you have a children's menu?

Avete un menu per bambini?

Ah-veh-tay oon men-oo pehr bahm-bee-nee?

Can I change my order?

Posso cambiare il mio ordine?

Pohs-soh kahm-bee-ah-ray eel mee-oh or-dee-nay?

Restrooms

Where is the bathroom?
Dove è il bagno?
Do-veh eh eel bah-nyoh?

Is there a toilet nearby?
C'è un bagno qui vicino?
Cheh oon bah-nyoh kwee vee-chee-noh?

Can I use the bathroom here?
Posso usare il bagno qui?
Pohs-soh oo-sah-reh eel bah-nyoh kwee?

Do you have a restroom for customers only?
Avete un bagno solo per i clienti?
Ah-veh-teh oon bah-nyoh soh-loh pehr ee klee-en-tee?

Where can I find a public toilet?
Dove posso trovare un bagno pubblico?
Do-veh pohs-soh troh-vah-reh oon bah-nyoh poob-blee-coh?

Is the bathroom accessible for wheelchairs?
Il bagno è accessibile per le sedie a rotelle?
Eel bah-nyoh eh ahk-chess-ee-bee-leh pehr leh seh-dee-eh ah roh-tel-leh?

Do I need a key to access the bathroom?
Mi serve una chiave per accedere al bagno?
Mee sehr-veh oo-nah kee-ah-veh pehr ahk-cheh-deh-reh ahl bah-nyoh?

Are there any free toilets around here?
Ci sono bagni gratuiti qui intorno?
Chee soh-noh bah-nyee grah-too-ee-tee kwee een-tor-noh?

How much does it cost to use the toilet?
Quanto costa usare il bagno?
Kwahn-toh koh-stah oo-sah-reh eel bah-nyoh?

Do you have a family bathroom?
Avete un bagno per famiglie?
Ah-veh-teh oon bah-nyoh pehr fah-mee-glee-eh?

Is there a baby changing facility in the bathroom?
C'è un fasciatoio nel bagno?
Cheh oon fah-shee-ah-toy-oh nehl bah-nyoh?

Where is the nearest restroom?
Dove è il bagno più vicino?
Do-veh eh eel bah-nyoh pyoo vee-chee-noh?

Can I have a toilet paper, please?
Posso avere della carta igienica, per favore?
*Pohs-soh ah-veh-reh del-lah kahr-tah ee-jee-eh-nee-kah,
pehr fah-voh-reh?*

Is there a charge for the toilet?
C'è una tariffa per il bagno?
Cheh oo-nah tah-ree-fah pehr eel bah-nyoh?

Can you direct me to the closest toilet, please?
Mi può indicare il bagno più vicino, per favore?
*Mee pwaw een-dee-kah-reh eel bah-nyoh pyoo vee-chee-noh,
pehr fah-voh-reh?*

Are the toilets cleaned regularly?
I bagni sono puliti regolarmente?
Ee bah-nyee soh-noh poo-lee-tee reh-goh-lahr-mehn-teh?

Is there a ladies' restroom nearby?
C'è un bagno per donne qui vicino?
Cheh oon bah-nyoh pehr doh-neh kwee vee-chee-noh?

Where is the men's restroom?
Dove è il bagno degli uomini?
Do-veh eh eel bah-nyoh deh-lee oo-mee-nee?

Do you need a coin to use the bathroom?
Serve una moneta per usare il bagno?
Sehr-veh oo-nah moh-neh-tah pehr oo-sah-reh eel bah-nyoh?

Are there any toilets for disabled persons?
Ci sono bagni per disabili?
Chee soh-noh bah-nyee pehr dee-sah-bee-lee?

Social Conversations

How are you?
Come stai?
Koh-meh stai?

What's your name?
Come ti chiami?
Koh-meh tee kee-ah-mee?

Where are you from?
Di dove sei?
Dee doh-veh seh-ee?

Do you speak English?
Parli inglese?
Pahr-lee een-gleh-seh?

I'm here on vacation.
Sono qui in vacanza.
Soh-noh kwee een vah-kahn-tsah.

What do you recommend visiting in this city?
Cosa consigli di visitare in questa città?
*Koh-sah kohn-see-lyee dee vee-zee-tah-reh een kweh-stah
chee-tah?*

Can we take a photo together?
Possiamo fare una foto insieme?
Poh-see-ah-moh fah-reh oo-nah foh-toh een-see-eh-meh?

What's your favorite food?
Qual è il tuo cibo preferito?
Kwah-leh eel too-oh chee-boh preh-feh-ree-toh?

Do you know a good place to eat here?
Conosci un buon posto dove mangiare qui?
Kohn-soh-shee oon bwon poh-stoh doh-veh mahn-jah-reh kwee?

What do you like to do in your free time?
Cosa ti piace fare nel tempo libero?
Koh-sah tee pee-ah-cheh fah-reh nehl tehm-poh lee-beh-roh?

How long have you been living here?
Da quanto tempo vivi qui?
Dah kwahn-toh tehm-poh vee-vee kwee?

Can you show me on the map?
Puoi mostrarmi sulla mappa?
Pwoh-ee moh-strahr-mee soo-lah mahp-pah?

I love this city!
Adoro questa città!
Ah-doh-roh kweh-stah chee-tah!

It's nice to meet you.
È un piacere conoscerti.
Eh oon pyah-cheh-reh koh-noh-shehr-tee.

Could you help me, please?
Potresti aiutarmi, per favore?
Poh-trehs-tee ah-yoo-tahr-mee, pehr fah-voh-reh?

What are the local customs?
Quali sono le usanze locali?
Kwah-lee soh-noh leh oo-sahn-tseh loh-kah-lee?

I'm looking for the museum.
Sto cercando il museo.
Stoh chehr-kahn-doh eel moo-seh-oh.

173

Where can I buy souvenirs?

Dove posso comprare souvenir?

Doh-veh pohs-soh kohm-prah-reh soo-veh-neer?

Can I try this, please?

Posso provare questo, per favore?

Pohs-soh proh-vah-reh kweh-stoh, pehr fah-voh-reh?

I would like to make a reservation.

Vorrei fare una prenotazione.

Vohr-reh-ee fah-reh oo-nah preh-noh-tah-tsyoh-neh.

Social network and phone numbers

Can I have your email address?
Can I have your email address?
Kan ay hav yor ee-mayl ad-dress?

What's your phone number?
Qual è il tuo numero di telefono?
Kwahl eh eel two-oh noo-meh-roh dee teh-leh-foh-noh?

Do you have a business card?
Hai un biglietto da visita?
Eye oon bee-lyet-toh dah vee-ze-tah?

Could you write down your contact info?
Potresti scrivere le tue informazioni di contatto?
Po-tres-tee skree-veh-reh leh twoo-eh een-for-mah-tsyoh-nee dee kon-tat-toh?

How can I find you on Facebook?
Come posso trovarti su Facebook?
Koh-meh pohs-soh troh-var-tee soo Fay-sbook?

What's your Instagram handle?
Qual è il tuo nome utente su Instagram?
Kwahl eh eel two-oh noh-meh oo-ten-teh soo Een-stah-gram?

Can you share your WhatsApp number?
Puoi condividere il tuo numero di WhatsApp?
Pwoy kon-dee-vee-deh-reh eel two-oh noo-meh-roh dee What-sApp?

Do you have a LinkedIn profile?
Hai un profilo LinkedIn?
Eye oon proh-fee-loh Lee-kin-den?

What is your home address?
Qual è il tuo indirizzo di casa?
Kwahl eh eel two-oh een-dee-ree-tssoh dee kah-sah?

How do I contact you for emergencies?
Come faccio a contattarti in caso di emergenza?
Koh-meh fat-cho ah kon-tat-tar-tee een kah-soh dee eh-mehr-jen-tsah?

Can you give me your Twitter username?
Puoi darmi il tuo nome utente di Twitter?
Pwoy dar-mee eel two-oh noh-meh oo-ten-teh dee Twee-ter?

Is there an email I can reach you at?
C'è un'email dove posso raggiungerti?
Cheh oo-neymayl doh-veh pohs-soh rahg-gyoon-jehr-tee?

Could I have your mobile number?
Potrei avere il tuo numero di cellulare?
Po-trey ah-veh-reh eel two-oh noo-meh-roh dee che-loo-lah-reh?

What's the best way to contact you?
Qual è il modo migliore per contattarti?
Kwahl eh eel moh-doh meel-yoh-reh pehr kon-tat-tar-tee?

Do you use any messaging apps?
Usi qualche app di messaggistica?
Oo-zee kwahl-keh app dee mes-sahj-jee-stee-kah?

Can I get your contact details for future reference?
Posso avere i tuoi dettagli di contatto per riferimento futuro?
Pohs-soh ah-veh-reh ee twoy deh-tah-glee dee kon-tat-toh
pehr ree-feh-reen-men-toh foo-too-roh?

What's your Snapchat username?
Qual è il tuo nome utente su Snapchat?
Kwahl eh eel two-oh noh-meh oo-ten-teh soo Snap-chat?

How can I add you on Telegram?
Come posso aggiungerti su Telegram?
Koh-meh pohs-soh adj-yoon-jehr-tee soo Teh-leh-gram?

Do you have a personal website?
Hai un sito personale?
Eye oon see-toh pehr-soh-nah-leh?

Can you give me your email for contact?
Puoi darmi la tua email per contatto?
Pwoy dar-mee lah two-ah eymayl pehr kon-tat-toh?

Sport

Where can I buy tickets for the football match?
Dove posso comprare i biglietti per la partita di calcio?
Do-veh pos-so kom-pra-re e bee-glee-et-tee per lah par-tee-tah dee kal-cho?

What time does the game start?
A che ora inizia la partita?
Ah keh oh-rah een-ee-tsyah lah par-tee-tah?

How do I get to the stadium?
Come faccio ad arrivare allo stadio?
Ko-meh fatch-cho ad ah-rree-vah-re al-lo sta-dee-oh?

Is there a sports bar nearby?
C'è un bar sportivo nelle vicinanze?
Cheh oon bar spor-tee-vo nel-le vee-chee-nahn-tseh?

Can I rent a bicycle here?
Posso noleggiare una bicicletta qui?
Pos-so no-lej-jah-re oo-nah bee-chee-klet-tah kwee?

Where can I find a running track?
Dove posso trovare una pista da corsa?
Do-veh pos-so tro-vah-re oo-nah pees-tah dah kor-sah?

Do you know a good place to swim?
Conosci un buon posto per nuotare?
Ko-no-shee oon bwon pos-toh per nwo-tah-re?

Is it safe to jog in this park?
È sicuro fare jogging in questo parco?
Eh see-koo-roh fa-re jog-ging een kwes-to par-ko?

Where can I watch the basketball game?
Dove posso guardare la partita di basket?
Do-veh pos-so gwahr-dah-re lah par-tee-tah dee bas-ket?

Can I join a yoga class here?
Posso unirmi a una classe di yoga qui?
Pos-so oo-neer-mee ah oo-nah klahs-seh dee yo-gah kwee?

How far is the nearest gym?
Quanto è distante la palestra più vicina?
Kwan-toh eh dees-tahn-teh lah pah-les-trah pyoo vee-chee-nah?

Do you have tennis courts?
Avete campi da tennis?
Ah-veh-te kam-pee dah teh-nees?

What sports are popular here?
Quali sport sono popolari qui?
Kwah-lee spor-t so-no po-po-lah-ree kwee?

Can I watch the match here?
Posso vedere la partita qui?
Pos-so veh-deh-re lah par-tee-tah kwee?

Are there any hiking trails nearby?
Ci sono sentieri per escursioni nelle vicinanze?
Chee so-no sen-tee-ree per es-kur-syo-nee nel-le vee-chee-nahn-tseh?

Where can I buy sports equipment?
Dove posso comprare attrezzature sportive?
Do-veh pos-so kom-pra-re at-tret-tsa-too-re spor-tee-veh?

Is there a place to play volleyball?
C'è un posto per giocare a pallavolo?
Cheh oon pos-to per joh-kah-re ah pal-la-vo-lo?

How can I get tickets for the swimming competition?
Come posso ottenere i biglietti per la competizione di nuoto?
Ko-meh pos-so ot-teh-neh-re e bee-glee-et-tee per lah kom-peh-tee-tsyoh-neh dee nwo-toh?

Are sports classes available for beginners?
Ci sono corsi sportivi per principianti?
Chee so-no kor-see spor-tee-vee per prin-chip-ee-ahn-tee?

Where is the closest bike rental?
Dove è il noleggio bici più vicino?
Do-veh eh eel no-lej-joh bee-chee pyoo vee-chee-noh?

Subway

How do I get to the nearest subway station?
Come faccio ad arrivare alla stazione della metropolitana più vicina?
Ko-meh fah-tcho ah-d ah-rree-vah-reh ah-lah stah-tsyoh-neh dehl-lah meh-troh-poh-lee-tah-nah pee-oo vee-chee-nah?

Is this the right way to the subway?
È questa la strada giusta per la metropolitana?
Eh kweh-stah lah strah-dah joo-stah pehr lah meh-troh-poh-lee-tah-nah?

Which line goes to the city center?
Quale linea va al centro città?
Kwah-leh lee-neh-ah vah ahl chen-troh chee-tah?

What is the last train time?
Qual è l'ultimo treno?
Kwah-leh lool-tee-moh treh-noh?

How many stops to the main station?
Quante fermate ci sono fino alla stazione principale?
Kwahn-teh fehr-mah-teh chee soh-noh feen-oh ah-lah stah-tsyoh-neh preen-chee-pah-leh?

Do I need to change lines for the museum?
Devo cambiare linea per il museo?
Deh-voh cahm-bee-ah-reh lee-neh-ah pehr eel moo-zeh-oh?

Where can I buy a subway ticket?
Dove posso comprare un biglietto della metropolitana?
Doh-veh pohs-soh kom-prah-reh oon bee-lyet-toh dehl-lah meh-troh-poh-lee-tah-nah?

Does this train go to the airport?
Questo treno va all'aeroporto?
Kweh-stoh treh-noh vah ahl-l'eh-roh-pohr-toh?

Can you show me on the map?
Puoi mostrarmi sulla mappa?
Pwoh-ee moh-strahr-mee soo-lah mahp-pah?

Is the subway station wheelchair accessible?
La stazione della metropolitana è accessibile in sedia a rotelle?
Lah stah-tsyoh-neh dehl-lah meh-troh-poh-lee-tah-nah eh ah-chess-see-bee-leh een seh-dee-ah ah roh-tehl-leh?

How do I use the ticket machine?
Come si usa la macchinetta dei biglietti?
Ko-meh see oo-sah lah mahk-kee-neh-tah dey bee-lyet-tee?

Where is the exit?
Dove è l'uscita?
Doh-veh eh loo-schee-tah?

Is there a map of the subway lines?
C'è una mappa delle linee della metropolitana?
Cheh oo-nah mahp-pah dehl-leh lee-neh-eh dehl-lah meh-troh-poh-lee-tah-nah?

Which way to the platform?
Da quale parte è il binario?
Dah kwah-leh pahr-teh eh eel bee-nah-ree-oh?

What time does the first train leave?
A che ora parte il primo treno?
Ah keh oh-rah pahr-teh eel pree-moh treh-noh?

Can I get a day pass?
Posso avere un abbonamento giornaliero?
Pohs-soh ah-veh-reh oon ahb-boh-nah-men-toh johr-nah-lee-eh-roh?

Are pets allowed on the subway?
Gli animali sono ammessi nella metropolitana?
Llee ah-nee-mah-lee soh-noh ahm-mehs-see nehl-lah meh-troh-poh-lee-tah-nah?

How do I get to the other side of the platform?
Come faccio ad arrivare dall'altra parte del binario?
Ko-meh fah-tcho ah-d ah-rree-vah-reh dahl-l'ahl-trah pahr-teh dehl bee-nah-ree-oh?

Do I need to stamp my ticket before boarding?
Devo timbrare il biglietto prima di salire?
Deh-voh teem-brah-reh eel bee-lyet-toh pree-mah dee sah-lee-reh?

Which exit should I take for the park?
Quale uscita devo prendere per il parco?
Kwah-leh oo-schee-tah deh-voh prehn-deh-reh pehr eel pahr-koh?

Supermarket

Where is the nearest supermarket?
Dove è il supermercato più vicino?
Do-veh eh eel soo-pehr-mehr-kah-toh pyoo vee-chee-noh?

Do you sell gluten-free products?
Vendete prodotti senza glutine?
Ven-deh-teh proh-doh-tee sen-zah gloo-tee-neh?

Can I get a shopping cart here?
Posso prendere un carrello qui?
Pohs-soh prehn-deh-reh oon kahr-rehl-loh kwee?

Where can I find fresh fruit?
Dove posso trovare frutta fresca?
Do-veh pohs-soh troh-vah-reh froot-tah freh-skah?

Are these eggs organic?
Queste uova sono biologiche?
Kwes-teh woh-vah soh-noh byoh-loh-ghee-keh?

How much is this per kilogram?
Quanto costa questo al chilogrammo?
Kwahn-toh koh-stah kwes-toh ahl kee-loh-grahm-moh?

Do you have plant-based milk?
Avete latte vegetale?
Ah-veh-teh laht-teh veh-jeh-tah-leh?

Is there a discount today?
C'è uno sconto oggi?
Cheh oon-oh skohn-toh oh-jee?

Can I taste this cheese?
Posso assaggiare questo formaggio?
Pohs-soh ah-ssah-jah-reh kwes-toh for-mah-joh?

Where are the frozen foods?
Dove sono i surgelati?
Do-veh soh-noh ee soor-jeh-lah-tee?

Do you accept credit cards?
Accettate carte di credito?
Ah-cheht-tah-teh kahr-teh dee kre-dee-toh?

Can I buy this in bulk?
Posso comprare questo alla rinfusa?
Pohs-soh kohm-prah-reh kwes-toh ahl-lah reen-foo-sah?

Where is the bakery section?
Dove è la sezione panetteria?
Do-veh eh lah sez-yoh-neh pah-net-teh-ree-ah?

Do you have any local wines?
Avete vini locali?
Ah-veh-teh vee-nee loh-kah-lee?

Are these snacks vegan?
Questi snack sono vegani?
Kwes-tee snahk soh-noh veh-gah-nee?

How do I use this self-checkout?
Come si usa questo self-service?
Koh-meh see oo-sah kwes-toh self-ser-vee-cheh?

Can I return a product here?
Posso restituire un prodotto qui?
Pohs-soh reh-stee-too-ee-reh oon proh-doh-toh kwee?

Where can I find bottled water?

Dove posso trovare acqua in bottiglia?

Do-veh pohs-soh troh-vah-reh ahk-kwah een boht-tee-lyah?

Is this fish fresh?

Questo pesce è fresco?

Kwes-toh peh-sheh eh freh-skoh?

Do you sell meat by the slice?

Vendete carne a fette?

Ven-deh-teh kahr-neh ah feht-teh?

Taxi

Can you take me to the airport?
Puoi portarmi all'aeroporto?
Pwoy por-tar-mee ahl-l'eh-roh-por-toh?

How much will it cost to get to the city center?
Quanto costa per arrivare al centro città?
Kwahn-toh koh-stah pehr ah-ree-vah-reh ahl chen-troh chee-tah?

Can you wait for me here?
Puoi aspettarmi qui?
Pwoy ah-speh-tar-mee kwee?

Do you accept credit cards?
Accetti carte di credito?
Ah-chet-tee kar-teh dee kre-dee-toh?

Could you please drive slower?
Potresti guidare più lentamente, per favore?
Poh-tres-tee gwee-dah-reh pyoo len-tah-men-teh, pehr fah-voh-reh?

Can I have a receipt, please?
Posso avere una ricevuta, per favore?
Pohs-soh ah-veh-reh oo-nah ree-che-voo-tah, pehr fah-voh-reh?

Could you help me with my luggage?
Potresti aiutarmi con i miei bagagli?
Poh-tres-tee ah-yoo-tar-mee kohn ee mee-ay bah-gahl-yee?

Do you know a good restaurant around here?
Conosci un buon ristorante qui vicino?
Kohn-noh-shee oon bwon rees-toh-rahn-teh kwee vee-chee-noh?

Is it far from here?
È lontano da qui?
Eh lon-tah-noh dah kwee?

Can we take this route instead?
Possiamo prendere questa strada invece?
Pohs-see-ah-moh pren-deh-reh kwes-tah strah-dah een-veh-cheh?

How long will the journey take?
Quanto tempo ci vuole per il viaggio?
Kwahn-toh tem-poh chee vwoh-leh pehr eel vee-ahj-joh?

Can you stop here, please?
Puoi fermarti qui, per favore?
Pwoy fehr-mar-tee kwee, pehr fah-voh-reh?

I'm in a hurry, can we go faster?
Ho fretta, possiamo andare più veloce?
Oh freh-tah, pohs-see-ah-moh ahn-dah-reh pyoo veh-loh-cheh?

Can you pick me up at 5 PM?
Puoi venirmi a prendere alle 5 di pomeriggio?
Pwoy veh-neer-mee ah pren-deh-reh ahl-leh cheen-kweh dee poh-meh-reej-joh?

Do you have a bigger car?
Hai una macchina più grande?
Eye oo-nah mah-keen-ah pyoo grahn-deh?

Can you recommend a sightseeing tour?
Puoi consigliarmi un tour turistico?
Pwoy kohn-see-lyar-mee oon toor too-ree-stee-koh?

Is tipping customary here?
È usanza dare la mancia qui?
Eh oo-zahn-zah dah-reh lah mahn-chah kwee?

Can I open the window?
Posso aprire la finestra?
Pohs-soh ah-pree-reh lah fee-nes-trah?

Do you know how to get to this address?
Sai come arrivare a questo indirizzo?
Sigh koh-meh ah-ree-vah-reh ah kwes-toh een-dee-ree-tzoh?

Can you drop me off near the metro station?
Puoi lasciarmi vicino alla stazione metro?
Pwoy lah-schar-mee vee-chee-noh ahl-lah stah-tsyoh-neh meh-troh?

Train Station

Where is the nearest train station?
Dove è la stazione ferroviaria più vicina?
Doh-veh eh lah stah-tsyoh-neh fehr-roh-vyah-ree-ah pee vee-chee-nah?

How do I get to the central station?
Come faccio ad arrivare alla stazione centrale?
Koh-meh fah-tchoh ad ah-rree-vah-reh ah-lah stah-tsyoh-neh chen-trah-leh?

What's the best way to the station?
Qual è il modo migliore per andare alla stazione?
Kwah-l eh eel moh-doh meel-yoh-reh pehr ahn-dah-reh ah-lah stah-tsyoh-neh?

Can you show me on the map how to get to the station?
Puoi mostrarmi sulla mappa come arrivare alla stazione?
Pwaw-ee moh-strahr-mee sool-lah mahp-pah koh-meh ah-rree-vah-reh ah-lah stah-tsyoh-neh?

Is it far to the train station?
È lontano la stazione ferroviaria?
Eh lon-tah-noh lah stah-tsyoh-neh fehr-roh-vyah-ree-ah?

Can I walk to the station?
Posso andare a piedi alla stazione?
Pohs-soh ahn-dah-reh ah pyeh-dee ah-lah stah-tsyoh-neh?

What time is the next train?
A che ora parte il prossimo treno?
Ah keh oh-rah pahr-teh eel prohs-see-moh treh-noh?

How much is a ticket to the station?
Quanto costa un biglietto per la stazione?
Kwahn-toh koh-stah oon bee-lyeh-toh pehr lah stah-tsyoh-neh?

Do I need to buy a ticket before boarding?
Devo comprare un biglietto prima di salire?
Deh-voh kohm-prah-reh oon bee-lyeh-toh pree-mah dee sah-lee-reh?

Which platform does the train to the station leave from?
Da quale binario parte il treno per la stazione?
Dah kwah-leh bee-nah-ree-oh pahr-teh eel treh-noh pehr lah stah-tsyoh-neh?

Is there a direct train to the station?
C'è un treno diretto per la stazione?
Cheh oon treh-noh dee-reht-toh pehr lah stah-tsyoh-neh?

Can I take a bus to the station?
Posso prendere un autobus per la stazione?
Pohs-soh prehn-deh-reh oon ow-toh-boos pehr lah stah-tsyoh-neh?

What time does the last train leave?
A che ora parte l'ultimo treno?
Ah keh oh-rah pahr-teh lool-tee-moh treh-noh?

How often do trains run to the station?
Ogni quanto partono i treni per la stazione?
Oh-nee kwahn-toh pahr-toh-noh ee treh-nee pehr lah stah-tsyoh-neh?

Do I need to change trains to get to the station?
Devo cambiare treno per arrivare alla stazione?
Deh-voh kahm-byah-reh treh-noh pehr ah-rree-vah-reh ah-lah stah-tsyoh-neh?

Where can I buy a ticket for the station?
Dove posso comprare un biglietto per la stazione?
Doh-veh pohs-soh kohm-prah-reh oon bee-lyeh-toh pehr lah stah-tsyoh-neh?

Can you help me with the timetable for the station?
Puoi aiutarmi con l'orario per la stazione?
Pwaw-ee ah-yoo-tahr-mee kohn loh-rah-ree-oh pehr lah stah-tsyoh-neh?

Is there a shuttle to the station?
C'è una navetta per la stazione?
Cheh oo-nah nah-veh-tah pehr lah stah-tsyoh-neh?

Where is the ticket machine?
Dove è la macchina biglietteria?
Doh-veh eh lah mahk-kee-nah bee-lyeh-teh-ree-ah?

Can I use a credit card to buy a ticket to the station?
Posso usare una carta di credito per comprare un biglietto per la stazione?
Pohs-soh oo-sah-reh oo-nah kahr-tah dee kre-dee-toh pehr kohm-prah-reh oon bee-lyeh-toh pehr lah stah-tsyoh-neh?

Traveling with Animals

Where is the nearest vet?
Dove è il veterinario più vicino?
Do-veh eh eel ve-te-ree-nah-ree-oh pyoo vee-chee-noh?

Do you have pet-friendly rooms?
Avete camere adatte agli animali?
Ah-veh-teh kah-meh-reh ahd-dah-teh ah-ly ah-nee-mah-lee?

Is there a dog park nearby?
C'è un parco per cani qui vicino?
Cheh oon par-koh pehr kah-nee kwee vee-chee-noh?

Can I buy dog food here?
Posso comprare cibo per cani qui?
Pohs-soh kom-prah-reh chee-boh pehr kah-nee kwee?

Do you sell cat litter?
Vendete lettiera per gatti?
Ven-deh-teh leh-tee-eh-rah pehr gah-tee?

Where can I walk my dog?
Dove posso portare a passeggio il mio cane?
Do-veh pohs-soh por-tah-reh ah pahs-seh-joh eel mee-oh kah-neh?

How do I find a pet store?
Come trovo un negozio di animali?
Koh-meh troh-voh oon neh-goh-tsyoh dee ah-nee-mah-lee?

Is there an emergency animal hospital?
C'è un ospedale per animali d'emergenza?
Cheh oon oh-speh-dah-leh pehr ah-nee-mah-lee deh-mehr-jen-tsah?

Can you recommend a pet sitter?
Puoi consigliare un dog sitter?
Pwoh-ee kon-seel-yah-reh oon dohg see-tter?

Are pets allowed in this area?
Gli animali sono ammessi in questa area?
Ly ah-nee-mah-lee soh-noh ahm-mes-see een kwes-tah ah-reh-ah?

Do you provide pet grooming services?
Offrite servizi di toelettatura per animali?
Ohf-free-teh sehr-vee-tsy dee toh-eh-leh-tah-too-rah pehr ah-nee-mah-lee?

Where can I buy a pet carrier?
Dove posso acquistare un trasportino per animali?
Do-veh pohs-soh ah-kwee-stah-reh oon trah-spor-tee-noh pehr ah-nee-mah-lee?

Are there any pet-friendly restaurants around?
Ci sono ristoranti che accettano animali qui intorno?
Chee soh-noh ree-stoh-rahn-tee keh ah-chet-tah-noh ah-nee-mah-lee kwee een-tor-noh?

Can I have a list of local pet services?
Posso avere un elenco dei servizi locali per animali?
Pohs-soh ah-veh-reh oon eh-len-koh deh-ee sehr-vee-tsy loh-kah-lee pehr ah-nee-mah-lee?

Is the beach dog-friendly?
La spiaggia è adatta ai cani?
Lah spee-ah-jah eh ahd-dah-tah ai kah-nee?

Can I take my pet on public transportation?
Posso portare il mio animale sui mezzi pubblici?
Pohs-soh por-tah-reh eel mee-oh ah-nee-mah-leh swee mehd-zee poob-blee-chee?

Do I need a pet passport?
Ho bisogno di un passaporto per l'animale?
Oh bee-zoh-nyoh dee oon pahs-sah-por-toh pehr lah-nee-mah-leh?

What are the local leash laws?
Quali sono le leggi locali sul guinzaglio?
Kwah-lee soh-noh leh leh-jee loh-kah-lee sool gween-tsah-lyoh?

Can you call a pet taxi for me?
Puoi chiamare un taxi per animali per me?
Pwoh-ee kyah-mah-reh oon tak-see pehr ah-nee-mah-lee pehr meh?

Do you have pet waste bags?
Avete sacchetti per i rifiuti degli animali?
Ah-veh-teh sak-keh-tee pehr ee ree-foo-tee deh-ly ah-nee-mah-lee?

Pet-friendly hotel
Hotel che accetta animali
Oh-tel keh ah-chet-tah ah-nee-mah-lee

Animal boarding
Pensione per animali
Pen-syoh-neh pehr ah-nee-mah-lee

Veterinary clinic
Clinica veterinaria
Klee-nee-kah veh-teh-ree-nah-ree-ah

Pet passport
Passaporto per animali
Pahs-sah-por-toh pehr ah-nee-mah-lee

Leash and collar
Guinzaglio e collare
Gween-dzah-lyoh eh kol-lah-reh

Pet carrier
Trasportino per animali
Trah-spor-tee-noh pehr ah-nee-mah-lee

Animal quarantine
Quarantena per animali
Kwah-ran-teh-nah pehr ah-nee-mah-lee

Vaccination records
Certificato di vaccinazione
Tcher-tee-fee-kah-toh dee vah-chee-nah-tsyoh-neh

No pets allowed
Vietato l'ingresso agli animali
Vee-eh-tah-toh leen-gres-soh ah-glee ah-nee-mah-lee

Pet food
Cibo per animali
Chee-boh pehr ah-nee-mah-lee

Dog park
Parco per cani
Par-koh pehr kah-nee

Animal behaviorist
Comportamentalista animale
Kom-por-tah-men-tah-lee-stah ah-nee-mah-leh

Pet sitter
Dog sitter
Dohg see-tter

Grooming services
Servizi di toelettatura
Ser-vee-tsy dee toh-eh-let-tah-too-rah

Microchip identification
Microchip identificativo
Mee-kroh-chip eeden-tee-fee-kah-tee-voh

Pet first aid
Pronto soccorso per animali
Pron-toh sok-kor-soh pehr ah-nee-mah-lee

Walking service
Servizio di passeggiata
Ser-vee-tsyoh dee pahs-sehd-jah-tah

Pet-friendly beach
Spiaggia che accetta animali
Spee-ahd-jah keh ah-chet-tah ah-nee-mah-lee

Litter box
Lettiera per animali
Let-tee-eh-rah pehr ah-nee-mah-lee

Spay/neuter service
Servizio di sterilizzazione
Ser-vee-tsyoh dee steh-ree-lee-tsa-tsyoh-neh

Vegetables

Carrot
Carota
Kah-roh-tah

Tomato
Pomodoro
Poh-moh-doh-roh

Lettuce
Lattuga
Lah-too-gah

Onion
Cipolla
Chee-poh-lah

Potato
Patata
Pah-tah-tah

Cucumber
Cetriolo
Cheh-tree-oh-loh

Pepper
Peperone
Peh-peh-roh-neh

Broccoli
Broccolo
Broh-koh-loh

Spinach

Spinaci
Spee-nah-chee

Zucchini
Zucchina
Tsook-kee-nah

Eggplant
Melanzana
Meh-lahn-zah-nah

Corn
Mais
Mah-ees

Mushroom
Fungo
Foon-goh

Garlic
Aglio
Ahl-yoh

Green beans
Fagiolini
Fah-joh-lee-nee

Cauliflower
Cavolfiore
Kah-vohl-fee-oh-reh

Asparagus
Asparagi
Ah-spah-rah-jee

Celery
Sedano
Seh-dah-noh

Beetroot
Barbabietola
Bar-bah-bee-eh-toh-lah

Cabbage
Cavolo
Kah-voh-loh

Vegans

Is this dish vegan?
Questo piatto è vegano?
Kwes-toh pyah-toh eh veh-gah-noh?

Do you have a vegan menu?
Avete un menù vegano?
Ah-veh-teh oon meh-noo veh-gah-noh?

Can you make this without dairy?
Potete preparare questo senza latticini?
Poh-teh-teh preh-pah-rah-reh kwes-toh sen-zah laht-tee-chee-nee?

Does this contain any animal products?
Contiene prodotti animali?
Kohn-tyeh-neh proh-doh-tee ah-nee-mah-lee?

Can I have the salad without cheese?
Posso avere l'insalata senza formaggio?
Pohs-soh ah-veh-reh leen-sah-lah-tah sen-zah for-mahj-joh?

Is the bread vegan?
Il pane è vegano?
Eel pah-neh eh veh-gah-noh?

What vegetable dishes do you have?
Quali piatti di verdure avete?
Kwah-lee pyah-tee dee vehr-doo-reh ah-veh-teh?

Can you suggest a vegan dessert?
Potete suggerire un dolce vegano?
Poh-teh-teh soo-jeh-ree-reh oon dol-che veh-gah-noh?

Do you use vegetable broth in this soup?
Usate brodo vegetale in questa zuppa?
Oo-zah-teh broh-doh veh-jeh-tah-leh een kwes-tah tzoop-pah?

Is there honey in this?
C'è miele in questo?
Cheh myeh-leh een kwes-toh?

Are the fries cooked in animal fat?
Le patatine sono fritte in grasso animale?
Leh pah-tah-tee-neh soh-noh free-tteh een grah-ssoh ah-nee-mah-leh?

Do you have almond milk?
Avete latte di mandorla?
Ah-veh-teh laht-teh dee man-dohr-lah?

Can this be made gluten-free?
Questo può essere fatto senza glutine?
Kwes-toh pwoh es-seh-reh fah-toh sen-zah gloo-tee-neh?

Do you have soy sauce?
Avete salsa di soia?
Ah-veh-teh sahl-sah dee soh-yah?

Is the pasta whole wheat?
La pasta è integrale?
Lah pah-stah eh een-teh-grah-leh?

Can I have a fruit salad?
Posso avere una macedonia?
Pohs-soh ah-veh-reh oo-nah mah-cheh-doh-nee-ah?

Is the wine vegan?
Il vino è vegano?
Eel vee-noh eh veh-gah-noh?

Are your smoothies made with dairy?
I vostri frullati sono fatti con latticini?
Ee voh-stree frool-lah-tee soh-noh fah-tee kohn laht-tee-chee-nee?

Do you offer any vegan snacks?
Offrite spuntini vegani?
Ohf-free-teh spoon-tee-nee veh-gah-nee?

Can I have vegetables instead of the side dish?
Posso avere verdure al posto del contorno?
Pohs-soh ah-veh-reh vehr-doo-reh ahl pohs-toh dehl kohn-tor-noh?

Vegetarians

Do you have vegetarian options?
Avete opzioni vegetariane?
Ah-veh-teh op-tsyoh-nee veh-jeh-tah-ree-ah-neh?

Is this dish made with any meat?
Questo piatto contiene carne?
Kwes-toh pyah-toh kohn-tyeh-neh kar-neh?

Can I have a salad without cheese?
Posso avere un'insalata senza formaggio?
Pohs-soh ah-veh-reh oon-een-sah-lah-tah sen-zah for-mah-joh?

What are the ingredients of this dish?
Quali sono gli ingredienti di questo piatto?
Kwah-lee soh-noh lyee een-greh-dyehn-tee dee kwes-toh pyah-toh?

Do you use animal fat in cooking?
Usate grassi animali nella cottura?
Oo-zah-teh grahs-see ah-nee-mah-lee nehl-lah koht-too-rah?

Can you make this dish without eggs?
Potete preparare questo piatto senza uova?
Poh-teh-teh preh-pah-rah-reh kwes-toh pyah-toh sen-zah oo-oh-vah?

Are there any vegetarian soups?
Ci sono zuppe vegetariane?
Chee soh-noh tzoop-peh veh-jeh-tah-ree-ah-neh?

Can I have the pasta with a vegetable sauce?
Posso avere la pasta con un sugo di verdure?
Pohs-soh ah-veh-reh lah pah-stah kohn oon soo-goh dee vehr-doo-reh?

Do you have vegan desserts?
Avete dolci vegani?
Ah-veh-teh dohl-chee veh-gah-nee?

Is the bread vegan?
Il pane è vegano?
Eel pah-neh eh veh-gah-noh?

What vegetarian dishes do you recommend?
Quali piatti vegetariani consigliate?
Kwah-lee pyah-tee veh-jeh-tah-ree-ah-nee kohn-see-lyah-teh?

Can I have a pizza without meat?
Posso avere una pizza senza carne?
Pohs-soh ah-veh-reh oon-ah peet-tsah sen-zah kar-neh?

Do the desserts contain gelatin?
I dolci contengono gelatina?
Ee dohl-chee kohn-ten-goh-noh jeh-lah-tee-nah?

Are the vegetable dishes cooked with meat stock?
I piatti di verdure sono cucinati con brodo di carne?
Ee pyah-tee dee vehr-doo-reh soh-noh koo-chee-nah-tee kohn broh-doh dee kar-neh?

Can I have a vegetable stir-fry?
Posso avere un saltato di verdure?
Pohs-soh ah-veh-reh oon sahl-tah-toh dee vehr-doo-reh?

Is there any meat in the vegetable soup?
C'è carne nella zuppa di verdure?
Cheh kar-neh nehl-lah tzoop-pah dee vehr-doo-reh?

Can you suggest a vegetarian wine?
Potete suggerire un vino vegetariano?
Poh-teh-teh soo-jeh-ree-reh oon vee-noh veh-jeh-tah-ree-ah-noh?

Does this vegetarian dish include dairy?
Questo piatto vegetariano include latticini?
Kwes-toh pyah-toh veh-jeh-tah-ree-ah-noh een-kloo-deh laht-tee-chee-nee?

Are there any meat flavors in this dish?
Ci sono sapori di carne in questo piatto?
Chee soh-noh sah-poh-ree dee kar-neh een kwes-toh pyah-toh?

Can I have a fruit salad for dessert?
Posso avere una macedonia per dolce?
Pohs-soh ah-veh-reh oon-ah mah-cheh-doh-nee-ah pehr dohl-cheh?

Wheelchair

Is this place wheelchair accessible?
Questo posto è accessibile in sedia a rotelle?
Iz thees plays weel-chehr ak-seh-suh-buhl?

Do you have a wheelchair ramp?
Avete una rampa per sedie a rotelle?
Doo yoo hav uh weel-chehr ramp?

Where is the elevator?
Dove è l'ascensore?
Whehr iz thuh el-uh-vay-tuhr?

Can I borrow a wheelchair?
Posso prendere in prestito una sedia a rotelle?
Kahn ahy bor-roh uh weel-chehr?

Is there a wheelchair-friendly restroom?
C'è un bagno accessibile alle sedie a rotelle?
Iz thehr uh weel-chehr-fren-lee reh-stroom?

Do you offer assistance for wheelchair users?
Offrite assistenza per gli utenti di sedia a rotelle?
Doo yoo of-fuhr uh-sis-tuhns fohr weel-chehr yoo-zuhrs?

How wide are the doorways for wheelchairs?
Quanto sono larghe le porte per le sedie a rotelle?
How wahyd ahr thuh dohr-wayz fohr weel-chehrs?

Is there accessible seating here?
Ci sono posti accessibili qui?
Iz thehr ak-seh-suh-buhl see-ting heer?

Can the table height accommodate a wheelchair?
L'altezza del tavolo può accomodare una sedia a rotelle?
Kahn thuh tay-buhl hahyt uh-kom-uh-dayt uh weel-chehr?

Are service animals allowed in here?
Gli animali di servizio sono ammessi qui?
Ahr sur-vis an-uh-muhls uh-loud ihn heer?

Is there a designated wheelchair area?
C'è un'area designata per le sedie a rotelle?
Iz thehr uh dez-ig-nay-tuhd weel-chehr ahr-uh?

Do you have accessible parking spots?
Avete posti auto accessibili?
Doo yoo hav ak-seh-suh-buhl pahr-king spots?

How do I get to the accessible entrance?
Come arrivo all'ingresso accessibile?
How doh ahy get toh thuh ak-seh-suh-buhl en-truhns?

Are there any steps to enter?
Ci sono gradini per entrare?
Ahr thehr en-ee steps toh en-tuhr?

Can someone help me with the doors?
Qualcuno può aiutarmi con le porte?
Kahn suhm-wuhn help me with thuh dohrz?

Where is the nearest accessible toilet?
Dove è il bagno accessibile più vicino?
Whehr iz thuh nee-ruhst ak-seh-suh-buhl toy-luht?

Is the path to the entrance smooth for wheelchairs?
Il percorso per l'ingresso è liscio per le sedie a rotelle?
Iz thuh path tuh thuh en-truhns smooth fohr weel-chehrs?

Do you have braille or tactile signs for the visually impaired?
Avete cartelli in braille o segnali tattili per i non vedenti?
Doo yoo hav brayl or tak-til signs fohr thuh vih-zhoo-uhl-ee im-payrd?

Can I get a map of the accessible facilities?
Posso ottenere una mappa delle strutture accessibili?
Kahn ahy get uh map of thuh ak-seh-suh-buhl fuh-sil-uh-tees?

Are there accessible emergency exits?
Ci sono uscite di emergenza accessibili?
Ahr thehr ak-seh-suh-buhl ih-mur-juhn-see ek-sits?

Women's Clothing Shopping

Do you have this in a smaller size?
Avete questo in una taglia più piccola?
Ah-veh-teh kwes-toh een oo-nah tah-lyah pyoo peek-koh-lah?

Can I try this on?
Posso provarlo?
Pohs-soh proh-vahr-loh?

Where is the fitting room?
Dove è il camerino?
Do-veh eh eel kah-meh-ree-noh?

How much does this dress cost?
Quanto costa questo vestito?
Kwahn-toh koh-stah kwes-toh veh-stee-toh?

Do you have these shoes in size ...?
Avete queste scarpe nel numero ...?
Ah-veh-teh kwes-teh skahr-peh nel noo-meh-roh...

Is this scarf silk?
Questa sciarpa è di seta?
Kwes-tah shahr-pah eh dee seh-tah?

I'm looking for a leather jacket.
Cerco una giacca di pelle.
Chair-koh oo-nah jah-kkah dee pehl-leh.

Where can I find accessories?
Dove posso trovare accessori?
Do-veh pohs-soh troh-vah-reh ahk-ches-soh-ree?

Do you sell sunglasses?
Vendete occhiali da sole?
Ven-deh-teh ok-kyah-lee dah soh-leh?

I need a belt.
Ho bisogno di una cintura.
Oh bee-zoh-nyoh dee oo-nah cheen-too-rah.

Can I get a discount?
Posso avere uno sconto?
Pohs-soh ah-veh-reh oo-noh skohn-toh?

This is too expensive for me.
Questo è troppo costoso per me.
Kwes-toh eh troh-poh koh-stoh-soh pehr meh.

Do you have any sales?
Avete saldi?
Ah-veh-teh sahl-dee?

I'm looking for a formal dress.
Cerco un vestito formale.
Chair-koh oon veh-stee-toh for-mah-leh.

Where can I find a swimsuit?
Dove posso trovare un costume da bagno?
Do-veh pohs-soh troh-vah-reh oon kohs-too-meh dah bahn-yoh?

Do you have this in another color?
Avete questo in un altro colore?
Ah-veh-teh kwes-toh een oon ahl-troh koh-loh-reh?

I would like to buy this hat.
Vorrei comprare questo cappello.
Vohr-ray kom-prah-reh kwes-toh kahp-pehl-loh.

Is this handbag leather?
Questa borsa è di pelle?
Kwes-tah bohr-sah eh dee pehl-leh?

I need earrings to match this necklace.
Ho bisogno di orecchini che abbinino a questa collana.
Oh bee-zoh-nyoh dee oh-rek-kee-nee keh ahb-bee-nee-noh ah kwes-tah koh-lah-nah.

Can you wrap this as a gift?
Puoi impacchettare questo come un regalo?
Pwoh-ee eem-pahk-keh-tah-reh kwes-toh koh-meh oon reh-gah-loh?

Women's Hairdresser

Where is the nearest women's hair salon?
Dove è il salone di bellezza per donne più vicino?
Whehr iz thuh nee-ruhst wuh-muhns hehr sah-lahn?

Do I need an appointment for a haircut?
Ho bisogno di un appuntamento per un taglio di capelli?
Doo ahy need uhn uh-poynt-muhnt fohr uhn hehr-kuht?

Can you do a hairstyle for a special occasion?
Puoi fare un'acconciatura per un'occasione speciale?
Kahn yoo doo uhn hehr-stahyl fohr uhn speh-shuhl oh-kay-zhuhn?

How much does a haircut and styling cost?
Quanto costa un taglio e piega?
How muhch duhz uhn hehr-kuht uhnd stahy-ling kohst?

Do you offer hair coloring services?
Offrite servizi di colorazione dei capelli?
Doo yoo oh-fuhr hehr kuhl-uhr-ing suhr-vuhs-ez?

Can I see a portfolio of your work?
Posso vedere un portfolio dei tuoi lavori?
Kahn ahy see uhn pohr-tuh-foh-lee-oh uhv yoor wuhrk?

How long will the appointment take?
Quanto tempo ci vorrà per l'appuntamento?
How lawng wihl thuh uh-poynt-muhnt tayk?

Do you use organic hair products?
Usate prodotti biologici per i capelli?
Doo yoo yooz oh-gan-ik hehr proh-duhktz?

Can you recommend a treatment for damaged hair?
Puoi consigliare un trattamento per capelli danneggiati?
Kahn yoo ruh-kuhm-end uhn truh-tuh-muhnt fohr dam-uhjd hehr?

Is there a hair stylist who specializes in curly hair?
C'è un parrucchiere specializzato in capelli ricci?
Iz thehr uhn hehr stahy-list hoo speh-shuh-lie-ziz ihn kuhr-lee hehr?

What are your opening hours?
Quali sono i vostri orari di apertura?
Wuht ahr yoor oh-puh-ning ow-uhrz?

Can I book an appointment online?
Posso prenotare un appuntamento online?
Kahn ahy buhk uhn uh-poynt-muhnt ohn-line?

Do you offer bridal hair services?
Offrite servizi per acconciature da sposa?
Doo yoo oh-fuhr bri-duhl hehr suhr-vuhs-ez?

How far in advance should I book?
Quanto tempo prima dovrei prenotare?
How fahr ihn uh-dvans shuhd ahy buhk?

Do you have a cancellation policy?
Avete una politica di cancellazione?
Doo yoo hav uhn kuhn-seh-lay-shuhn puh-lih-see?

Can you fix a bad haircut from another salon?
Potete sistemare un taglio di capelli sbagliato fatto da un altro salone?
Kahn yoo fihks uhn bad hehr-kuht fruhm uhn-uh-thuhr sah-lahn?

Do you sell hair care products?
Vendete prodotti per la cura dei capelli?
Doo yoo sehl hehr kehr proh-duhktz?

Are your hair dyes ammonia-free?
I vostri colori per capelli sono senza ammoniaca?
Ahr yoor hehr dahyz uh-moh-nee-uh-free?

Can I have a consultation before deciding?
Posso avere una consulenza prima di decidere?
Kahn ahy hav uhn kuhn-suhl-tay-shuhn bee-fohr dih-sahy-ding?

What hair treatments do you offer for dry hair?
Quali trattamenti per capelli secchi offrite?
Wuht hehr truh-tuh-muhnts doo yoo oh-fuhr fohr dry hehr?

Made in the USA
Middletown, DE
30 August 2024

59999643R00119